Inspired *to* Write

Readings and tasks to develop writing skills

TEACHER'S MANUAL

JEAN WITHROW
GAY BROOKES
MARTHA CLARK CUMMINGS

CAMBRIDGE
UNIVERSITY PRESS

CAMBRIDGE UNIVERSITY PRESS
Cambridge, New York, Melbourne, Madrid, Cape Town,
Singapore, São Paulo, Delhi, Mexico City

Cambridge University Press
32 Avenue of the Americas, New York, NY 10013–2473, USA

www.cambridge.org
Information on this title: www.cambridge.org/9780521537124

First published 2005
5th printing 2013

Printed in the United States of America

A catalog record for this publication is available from the British Library.

ISBN 978-0-521-53712-4 paperback

Table *of* Contents

Introduction

The approach

The goal of **Inspired *to* Write** is to encourage students to think and inspire them to write by exposing them to well-written, provocative texts. **Inspired *to* Write** uses a collaborative and student-based approach and gives students tools to develop their writing and reading skills. Students respond to original texts, to words and meaning, to images and associations, and to the way texts are written. They write about the texts they read and related topics, exchange feedback about their writing, and revise some of their writing. Constant interaction about meaning and ideas with text, authors, and classmates helps students develop their language and thinking in general and their writing in particular.

The book is intended for adults and young adults. It may be used by ESL students at the post intermediate level, by high school students preparing to write at the college level, or by anyone who wants to develop from a basic writer to a more accomplished writer.

The instructor's role

This is a student-centered book, and the role of the instructor is often implied. Some of your tasks will include the following: setting up groups or pairs; answering questions about activities, readings, and instructions for writing; and structuring and facilitating class discussion to help make sense out of sometimes conflicting interpretations.

One thing to remember is that we think there are many acceptable ways to respond to or interpret a reading and many ways to write in response to them. We see your role as facilitator and coach. To this end, you may prod and encourage, suggest and question. But primarily we hope you will provide a student-centered classroom where students feel free to express themselves honestly, ask questions, make tentative propositions, and respond openly to what they read and to each other.

UNIT 1

Becoming

UNIT PREVIEW (pages 2–3)

A Make connections

This task introduces the concept of freewriting. Students are given guidelines and asked to freewrite about the opening quotation by Joan Sauro. However, some students may find this quotation to be too abstract, so to introduce freewriting, we suggest that students freewrite about a simpler topic first and then go back to try freewriting again about the given topic. Simpler topics include: *Yesterday, Last night, My weekend, My favorite place,* and *I can't write today because . . .*

Tell students that the important thing about freewriting is to keep going, that there is no need to be logical or to stay with the topic you start with. Another important point about freewriting is giving students the right not to share their writing. If students are expected to let go, to write whatever is on their minds, they shouldn't be forced to share. Some students enjoy writing for an audience and do their freewriting with a particular peer in mind. Others, however, find that their freewriting leads them into dangerous places. So give students the choice about whether they want to share.

Depending on the level of the students, once you have introduced freewriting and allowed them to try it for five minutes or so, invite them to finish the sentence they are working on and put down their pens. If they don't want to share what they've written, ask them to tell their partner what the experience of freewriting was like for them. Some students will find it very liberating, others will say it is very annoying at first, that they don't have time to think, that they want to reread what they have written, that they would have written something better if they had been able to stop and reflect. It helps to remind students from time to time that freewriting is a way to generate ideas, a way to find out things we didn't know were on our minds. It should never be considered a finished product.

Once students have had a chance to practice (if necessary), read the Joan Sauro quote aloud to them. Explain, depending on the level of your students, that everyone we meet in our lives is always with us. Then, if students are still puzzled, suggest that they try to freewrite about all the places they have ever visited, or all the books they have ever read, or every person they have ever loved. One of those ideas usually appeals to them. Again, after five to seven minutes, depending on how much energy you sense is going into their writing, stop them and invite them to share.

Before sharing, make the following suggestions to your students: Tell the readers to just start reading aloud, not to apologize, explain, criticize, or stall. We have all written something imperfect and unfinished. If something is too personal, tell them they can skip it. Tell the listeners to listen carefully and when the readers have finished to tell them what they understood, not what they thought was good or bad.

B Make a map of your life

The "map of your life" activity can be quite engaging. Crayons and colored markers encourage elaborate and detailed "maps," although pens and pencils work fine. The activity of drawing can take at least twenty minutes. Some students may even ask if they can redo their maps at home or on a computer. These maps may include language as well as pictures and other graphic representations.

The sharing of maps takes a minimum of 10 minutes and can go on longer, as you direct. You might put some of the maps on the wall or show them to the whole class. Save a few of them as examples to inspire your next class.

Again, ask your students to freewrite for five minutes about their own maps or what they discovered from looking at their classmates' maps. Then have them read the *Kernel Sentences* toolbox and write a kernel sentence about their freewriting.

C Preview Unit 1

Give the students 10 minutes to look through the unit and another 10 minutes to discuss the connections in their groups. While the unit focuses on who we are, where we come from, our family, cultural origins and values, many other possible connections can be made. Remind students that there are no wrong answers and that all opinions and connections made in the class are valued and respected.

Family Origins

Brothers (pages 4–6)
Bret Lott

This reading recreates the sensation in words of watching an old home movie. In this age of digital cameras and cell phones with built-in movie cameras, the concept of a faded home movie may require some explanation.

BEFORE READING (page 4)

Think about the title

Make sure your students understand that *conflict* can mean something mental as well as physical, between two individuals as well as between forces or countries.

Usually pre-reading activities are done in writing. This one is not. Some students, however, may be more comfortable with making a list or some notes before discussing a childhood incident with a partner. Consider this option.

AFTER READING (page 5)

A Retell the story

Again, the emphasis here is on telling instead of writing. The students will notice that a lot of verbs are repeated: *lean, speak, kick, splash, look, laugh.* The pinch, of course, is the turning point in the story.

B Make a picture quiz

This activity is designed for students who can understand a situation better visually than they can verbally. Many of the same words will come up that came up in the previous task, along with *flinch, pinch, squeeze, grab, grimace, shiver, cry, cut,* and *wave off.*

HOW IT'S WRITTEN (page 6)

Notice verbs

This activity can take at least 20 minutes, depending on the level of your class. However, once students get the hang of it, they see that the action is described in the present tense to dramatize it, and that there are some powerful verbs used to describe the actions that take place in the story.

TOPICS FOR WRITING (page 6)

Choose one topic to write about

If students choose the first topic, they may have to work from memory, as they may not have a photograph with them. Topic 3 could be turned into a research topic for more advanced level students. Much has been written about the effects of birth order on people's lives. An online search of "birth order" found this Web site: <http://childdevelopmentinfo.com/ development/birth_order.htm>.

AFTER WRITING (page 6)

Share your writing

All of the activities in **Inspired *to* Write** work best if they are modeled for the students, not just once but repeatedly. One way to start is to read aloud a piece written by a student from a previous semester and ask your students to tell you what they like about it as if you were that student. Another option is to have two students model the procedure for the whole class. In our classes, we constantly remind our students that writers need encouragement and support in order to keep writing, especially at the outset. We recommend telling students about some advice given by Donald M. Murray, a Pulitzer-prize winning journalist and author of several books on the craft of writing. Murray has said that we should only talk to people about our writing who make us want to hurry back to our desks and write more, and that we should be those kinds of people for each other.

....

The Brown Hen (pages 7–11)
Esmeralda Santiago

This childhood memory, besides having a strong narrative, is abundant in sensory detail and colorful vocabulary. Students may wish to emulate the author's powers of observation and may come to appreciate her effort to use a wide range of words to paint a picture.

BEFORE READING (page 7)

Make a list

When introducing the *Brainstorming a List* toolbox, try to get everyone involved with the activity in order to demonstrate the power of collective brainstorming. Students can first share with a partner, then with a group, then with the whole class. Sometimes, for this particular brainstorming session, there is competition over whose disobedience was the most serious!

AFTER READING (pages 9–10)

A Respond to the reading

The *Response Questions* toolbox is a useful starting place for responding to a reading or to another student's writing. "What do you understand the reading to say?" can be taken on a literal or a figurative level. That is, students can simply retell the story, or they can talk about power relations and conflicts in families. In answer to "How does the reading make you feel?" try to accept all answers, even from those who say "bored" or "annoyed," but then ask the students to explain exactly what was so boring or annoying about what they read. Do not accept such negative answers when students are responding to each others' work, however. In answer to "What does the reading make you think about?" some students will tell stories about their own siblings; some will recall the first reading in the book; and some will think about what they wrote for the previous reading.

B Analyze the story

This story is fairly straightforward with few characters, and the major events are clear-cut, so steps 1–3 can be done quickly. To help students complete the chart, however, they may need to be supplied with the names of feelings: dismay, fear, panic, anxiety, misgiving, worry, bravery, courage, anger, awe, esteem, respect, contempt, scorn, annoyance, irritation, exasperation, rage, indignation, fury, reproach, shame, embarrassment, and guilt.

Possible answers (page 10)

Events	Characters	Feelings
• found stones	Delsa, Negi	bored, restless
• walked, then ran around the hen	Delsa, Negi	mischievous, wicked
• scolded and punished Negi	Mami	angry
• ran home	Negi and Delsa	guilty, offended
• sobbed	Delsa	guilty, scared
• raked the dirt	Papi	indifferent
• screamed, pushed Delsa	Negi	in a rage, furious
• fought each other	Delsa, Negi	angry, hurt by parents' seeming lack of comfort

HOW IT'S WRITTEN (pages 10–11)

A Practice a sensory awareness exercise

Although this exercise can be time-consuming, its effects on student writing are immediate and rewarding. Using their senses and including appeals to the reader's senses makes their writing dramatically more powerful. Students notice this and are thrilled with the results.

B Find examples of sensory details

Many images in this reading fit into more than one category. Every sentence is filled with appeals to the readers' senses.

Possible answers (page 11)

Sound: the creaky joints of the furniture; the soft clucking of the hen; her voice quivered with fury [Mami]

Taste: eggs; the scent of cooking spices

Smell: a stack of new floorboards; latrine; the scent of cooking spices

Touch: baked in the sun; their worn surfaces scarred; their joints loose and creaky; small stones; a brown hen sat on her nest, her wings fluffed around the eggs; [the hen] buried her head into her feathers the way a turtle crawls into a shell; [Mami] knuckled me hard on the head. I ran home, rubbing the bump that was forming under my hair

Sight: Papi dragged our belongings out to the yard; all of the description of the hen; the description of Mami's expression compared to the hen's, on pages 9 and 10

TOPICS FOR WRITING (page 11)

Choose one topic to write about

Again, the *Using Your Senses* toolbox on page 10 will do wonders for these topics. Topic 3 allows the students to use their senses in imaginative ways.

AFTER WRITING (page 11)

Share your writing

It takes practice and discipline for students to tell what they understood and make statements such as: "I understand you loved the house you grew up in," or "I understand you were surprised by the things students do in the cafeteria." Typically they would rather ask questions or give reactions. You will want to monitor pairs to make sure they follow the instructions. Also, warn students not to expect complete communication.

....

Memory: My Mother (pages 12–15)
Amy Tan

This is a hard-hitting emotional piece about the author's relationship with her mother that evokes reactions and stories, sometimes surprising ones, from even the quietest students.

BEFORE READING (page 12)

Gather ideas about the topic

Another toolbox, *Clustering,* is introduced here. Students appreciate doing this activity on the whiteboard together the first time. If there is space, you can have several groups working simultaneously and then compare the results, or use overhead transparencies, or use computer graphics if you have the access and your students have the skills.

AFTER READING (page 14)

A Respond to the reading

Encourage students to keep the *Response Questions* toolbox (page 9) in front of them as they write.

B Understand the time periods

The author divided the reading into three sections. She was 16 in the first, second, and part of the third paragraph. She was 47 in the remainder of the text until the last paragraph, which takes place in the present. These are important turning points in Tan's relationship with her mother, moments when important words were spoken.

C Think about a quote

Usually, after reading this quote, students discuss forgiveness in general and specific instances of forgiveness in their lives. They also write about times when they were hurt or when they hurt someone.

HOW IT'S WRITTEN (pages 14–15)

Think about describing people

In this activity, we hope the students will learn that by describing very precise, concrete, specific actions and quoting someone's exact words, writers are able to give very vivid pictures of the people they are describing.

Possible answers to Step 1 (page 14)

> **Words and phrases:** . . . her chin raised, her lips stretched in a crazy smile. 'O.K., maybe I die,' she said. 'Then I no longer be your mother!'; Sometimes she actually tried to kill herself, by running into the street, holding a knife to her throat; . . . she would not speak to me. She tormented me, acted as if she had no feelings for me whatsoever; . . . she criticized me, humiliated me in front of others, forbade me to do this or that . . .

TOPICS FOR WRITING (page 15)

Choose one topic to write about

The first topic evokes some very sad, often heartfelt stories, as does the second. The third topic usually evokes angrier writing.

AFTER WRITING (page 15)

Give feedback

It is very important to model this process for the students, not once but repeatedly. The bravest way to do this is to share a piece of your own writing, your freewriting, for instance, and ask them to respond as instructed in the *Reader's Response Feedback* toolbox. You can do this aloud so that a discussion can follow. Tell the students that "say what you understand" just means tell the writer what you remember about what she wrote. All writers need to know that they were heard and understood. The final point, "Say one or more things you would like to know more about," helps the writer to continue developing this piece of writing.

There Was Rice at Every Meal (pages 16–20)

Eric Koji Stowe

This is a touching essay, if a bit formulaic, on a topic that students identify with – family and family life. The author is not only a student but also loving toward his family – making it easy to like him and want to write like him.

BEFORE READING (page 16)

Make a personal connection

There are very few places in the world where people will claim that their parents come from exactly the same kind of background in every way (ethnically, culturally, socially, economically, etc.), but if you are teaching in one of them, suggest they write about anyone they know who is married to someone who is different in some way.

AFTER READING (page 18)

A Look for topics in the reading

Stowe raises a lot of topics in this reading. Some of them are: differences in race, physical size, eating habits, culture, language, religion, and philosophy; long-lasting monogamous marriages; respect; demonstrating affection; traveling to find one's roots.

B Write a discussion letter

If you have access to computers and students have e-mail accounts or access to a computer network system, they can send these letters to four other students via e-mail, with copies to you, and have the discussion electronically.

HOW IT'S WRITTEN (pages 18–19)

Learn about the essay

After reading *The Essay* toolbox, the obvious answer to the question in step 2 is that this reading is an example of Type 1.

TOPICS FOR WRITING (page 19)

Choose one topic to write about

Depending on the makeup of your student group, there may be some very sharp opinions expressed for the second topic. You may need to take this into account when students work in groups and share their writing later.

AFTER WRITING (page 20)

Share your writing

If you let students choose their own group mates for their writing circles, they will usually choose people they feel most safe and comfortable with. This is another activity that benefits very much from being modeled.

FAMILY ORIGINS: REVISION (page 21)

A Revise one piece of writing

After the students read the *Drafting* toolbox, they are instructed to reread all of the drafts they wrote for this section and to choose one piece to revise. Some teachers wait until this stage of the writing process, after the second draft, to make extensive comments on student papers.

B Share your writing

For the students, choosing one writer's work and sharing it with the whole class can be a powerful and moving experience. If the writer himself is too shy to read his piece aloud, it is OK to let another student read it for him.

Between Two Cultures

Safe (pages 22–25)

Cherylene Lee

This is a funny excerpt about overprotective parents. The excerpt may seem particularly Chinese, but it crosses all cultures by reminding us of times when our parents or guardians protected us from danger.

BEFORE READING (page 22)

Think about the topic

The issue of safety is a popular one for international students newly arrived in the United States, and this freewriting may provoke a wave of anxiety, in which case the discussion of how to protect oneself may become prolonged. On the other hand, in some places in the world (rural Japan, for instance), it has been difficult for students to think of times when they felt unsafe.

AFTER READING (pages 23–24)

A Understand the reading

A closer look at the text reveals that some of the fears (going out at night) and precautions (not taking a shower after dinner) are much more rational than others. It is interesting for students to discover that the mother seems to fear only for her own and her daughter's physical safety, while the father wants to protect his material possessions.

Possible answers (page 23)

Who	Fears	Precautions
Mother	Darkness	No going out after dark
	Showering after dinner leads to cramps	No showering after dinner
	Drowning in the shower	Maybe no showering at all
	Walking home alone	Walk with at least three other girls
	Bad influence from hanging around with "fast" girls	Watch out
Father	Getting dents in his parked car	Leaves two spaces on each side
	Fear of being robbed in a grocery store	Won't go into a grocery store if he's the first or last customer
	Getting germs from eating out	Wipes all implements (chopsticks, glasses, etc.)
	Fear of his tailor shop being robbed	Has more locks and alarms than the bank

B Make a personal connection

Again, depending on where you are teaching, these answers can vary widely.

C Think about a quote

Usually students come up with two possible effects: either the writer became fearful herself, or, in reaction, she became reckless.

HOW IT'S WRITTEN (page 24)

Look for details

Possible words: *safe, caution, weren't sure, protect, precautions, for fear of, for fear, maximum protection,* and *run for help.* There are other readings, such as Russell Baker's "Becoming a Writer" (pages 59–60) and Jamaica Kincaid's "A Walk to the Jetty" (pages 83–84), where the powerful effect of repetition and the use of synonyms is also pointed out. You can refer back to this piece at that time.

Possible answers (page 24)

The names of feelings students have come up with include: fear of the dark, fear of cramps, fear of bad things happening at an early age, fear of robbers, fear of a dented car, fear of germs, and fear of not arriving safely.

Two possible clues that explain the narrator's feelings: the narrator's parents married late in life and were having financial difficulties.

TOPICS FOR WRITING (page 24)

Choose one topic to write about

The first and second topics lead toward personal narrative. The third, however, leads the students toward a more academic approach to the topic.

AFTER WRITING (page 25)

Share your writing

Make sure the students reread the toolbox. Monitor how they are doing and model this approach again if necessary.

. . . .

I Answer to "Elaine" (pages 25–28)

M. Elaine Mar

This excerpt from a memoir presents a growing-up conflict, in this case growing up in America, between a daughter and mother. The daughter becomes increasingly frustrated with her mother's cultural ways. In this excerpt they grow apart, with the daughter gaining an "empty" American identity while creating a breach in the family.

BEFORE READING (page 25)

Think about the title and the author

According to the author, she was a "paper daughter" because she only really knew her father through the letters they exchanged after she had moved to the United States. Mar, who considers herself a "working-class paper daughter" who went to Harvard, also thinks she is tied to the world of writing and academia by pieces of paper: a high school diploma, her British passport, and her American Social Security card.

Your students will probably not think of these things, but they may come up with much more interesting interpretations. One of our students wrote: "I think the phrase 'paper daughter' means that her parents are like the paper the writer uses. If we wish we can write on it or we can tear it or in case of importance, we can preserve it safely."

AFTER READING (pages 26–27)

A Respond to the reading

The *Double Entry Response* toolbox introduces this concept. Generally speaking, students like to copy down the exact words they read on the left side of the paper, sometimes just for the joy of getting it right. This is fine. Demonstrating some possible responses to a reading is helpful here.

B Check your understanding

Some students may have trouble with individual words and phrases, others with concepts. One student had trouble understanding what the mother meant when she said, "If I weren't so fat, how would you know you were thin?"

C List the conflicts

In some ways Mar felt in conflict with her mother: how to dress, how to interpret their roles in life (this is relevant to the next reading), the legalities of certain actions, gender roles.

HOW IT'S WRITTEN (page 28)

Look for details

Possible answers (page 28)

> **Details underlined in paragraph two:** skirts sewn out of restaurant flour sacks; acrylic sweaters from Kmart; hand-me-downs; taupe nylon stockings; gauzy, discolored legs

TOPICS FOR WRITING (page 28)

Choose one topic to write about

You may want to read and discuss the *Writer's Tip* with students before having them start writing.

AFTER WRITING (page 28)

Share your writing

Monitor the groups to make sure listeners understand their task.

. . . .

Translating for Parents Means Growing Up Fast (pages 29–33)

Misha Kratochvil

The headline (the title) of this article tells all, an example of a general statement that covers the examples. The various points of view in the article show how immigrant kids are often used as the bridge to the new world for parents. The article presents ways these kids suffer as well as how they benefit.

BEFORE READING (page 29)

A Ask questions before reading

Some possible questions: Translating what? Where? When? Why? Is it embarrassing when your parents don't speak the language of the country where you live? Do you feel like the girl in "The First Day" on page 78? Does it negatively affect your life to translate for your parents?

B Think about the topic

Possible answers (page 29)

> **Possible roles for parents:** teachers, authority figures, disciplinarians, guardians, guards, caretakers, nurturers, problem-solvers, protectors, watchdogs, rule makers, governors, buffers
>
> **Possible roles for children:** learners, rule breakers, entertainers, players, dependent, needy, obedient, rebellious

AFTER READING (pages 31–32)

A Answer your pre-reading questions

Answers will vary depending on the questions that the students came up with initially. It is always fun for students to test each other's reading comprehension by asking their own, not the book's, questions.

B Freewrite a response

This suggestion led one of us to a lengthy freewriting session about translating for her parents that developed into a short story. We tell you this because we never know where freewriting is going to lead us, and to remind you that it's always good to freewrite with your students and to share your freewriting with them.

C Restate general statements

This activity is the first that relates to paraphrasing, which is explained more thoroughly in the *Quoting and Paraphrasing* toolbox on page 135.

Possible answers (page 32)

> 1 According to sociologists, family dynamics are turned upside down when children interpret for their parents.
> 2 The tradition among American immigrant children translating for their parents has disadvantages.
> 3 According to psychologists, children's self-esteem may grow stronger over the years, but the immediate effect is stress as well as psychological and practical problems.
> 4 Other smaller problems are provoked by children translating for parents, including every teen's downfall: embarrassment.

HOW IT'S WRITTEN (page 32)

Find supporting examples

The point of this activity, which hopefully students will write about in their logs, is that when you support a general statement with examples, authority is brought to your writing, making it more believable.

Possible answers (page 32)

> **General statement:** The duties can bring great strain.
>
> **Example:** The boy who could not translate the word *cancer.*
>
> **General statement:** . . . The dynamics of the typical family become inverted.
>
> **Example:** The girl who urged her mother to be more independent and less shy at work.

TOPICS FOR WRITING (pages 32–33)

Choose one topic to write about

For the first topic, students could contrast themselves with the parents, the children, the immigrants, the psychologists, the translators, the grandmother, the teachers, the shopkeepers, or the doctors. The second and third topics take students a step closer to academic writing. When students revise these pieces, they may want to organize the writing in the more typical academic way, by putting the general statements first, followed by the examples.

AFTER WRITING (page 33)

Share your writing

Students are usually pleased to find similarities and intrigued by differences. They learn, we hope, the importance of supporting evidence.

....

No Comprendo (pages 33–37)
Barbara Mujica

This opinion piece about bilingual education is sharp and pointed. It begins and ends with a personal story and weaves supporting details around and through it. It ends up authoritatively coming down on the side of students' needing "English more than bilingualism."

For your students who know no Spanish, translate the title. "I don't understand." You might also want to point out that "Spanglish" is a combination of Spanish and English so they don't get distracted by that term.

BEFORE READING (page 33)

Think about the topic

Students should be familiar with this predicting strategy now. Additional questions are included to guide their discussion.

AFTER READING (page 35)

A Find the main idea

Gradually, as students work through the first unit, we introduce them to important concepts in academic writing. Here, we focus on the importance of the main idea.

Possible answer (page 35)

| **Author's main idea:** Bilingual education doesn't work.

B Respond to the reading

Students have varied and changing thoughts and feelings about the issues raised in this editorial. This response could be the beginning of an engaging discussion about issues of bilingual education, bilingualism, language and society, and the like.

HOW IT'S WRITTEN (pages 35–36)

Analyze the essay

Descriptive outlining is a technique that was inspired by Kenneth Bruffee's book, *A Short Course in Writing*, where you will find a much more detailed explanation and many examples.

Possible answers (page 36)

Main idea: _____

	What each paragraph says	What each paragraph does
Par. 1	The niece was upset; the aunt wondered why.	Describes the situation, sets up a question to be answered
Par. 2	The niece came as a child; she was still unsure of her English.	Tells the niece's background, gives her history
Par. 3	The niece's school kept her in a Spanish-speaking classroom.	Begins a rationale for the niece's insecurity in English
Par. 4	The school is really run in "Spanglish," not English.	Describes the problem from another perspective
Par. 5	Students aren't getting English skills because of Bilingual Education.	Explains the problem from a historical perspective
Par. 6	Data show that Hispanics have a high dropout rate due to insufficient English skills.	Adds further support to the point that English is essential
Par. 7	Putting students in Spanish language settings in America may be kind but not helpful.	Makes a secondary point in support of the main point, synthesizes her idea
Par. 8	The niece decided to attend a college in Miami to stay in a Spanish language setting.	Provides an ironic conclusion to the niece's story and to the essay

TOPICS FOR WRITING (pages 36–37)

Choose one topic to write about

For students who do the first topic, refer them to the reading "The Model Medic" on pages 124–125 for an example of a profile as well as to the activities that follow it for interviewing techniques. A good suggestion for the second topic is to make sure students support generalizations with examples, as Mujica does. The third topic is related to the title of the essay, not the essay itself. It asks students to write about a time when they did not understand.

AFTER WRITING (page 37)

Share your writing

These questions are meant to reinforce the importance of having a main idea.

BETWEEN TWO CULTURES: REVISION (pages 38–39)

A Choose one piece of writing

This second revision section invites the students to revise one of the four pieces they wrote. If they have already revised them once, please remind them that professional writers revise their work dozens of times.

B Think about titles

From the discussion about titles, students should come away with the notion that the title provides the reader with a frame, or a way to interpret what follows. Titles can be informative, humorous, summative, or intertextual. When students look at the titles in the table of contents they may express interest in other readings in the book. Some actually read them before they are assigned!

Before students do steps 3–5, you may want to have them look first at the *Skimming* toolbox on page 161.

C Revise

It's possible that choosing a new title will change the focus of the piece. Sometimes this is exciting for student writers. They realize there are other ideas to be mined.

D Share your writing

As students listen to each student's piece of writing, have them think about the appropriateness of the piece's title.

Five New Words at a Time (pages 40–43)
Yu-Lan (Mary) Ying

This essay describing a young immigrant's experience of learning English with her mother's help was written for a contest entitled, "A Woman I Admire." It also describes the writer's language learning experience and offers an effective language learning strategy. Thus, in a sense, it has two themes.

BEFORE READING (page 40)
Think about the topic

Possible answers (page 40)

> **Some possible connections:** we admire heroes; the girl who wrote the essay won a prize; we admire prizewinners.

AFTER READING (pages 41–42)
A Respond to the reading

Reactions are varied, but most people understand that the mother is a hero. Many students are reminded of their own language learning experience.

B Make a visual representation

This is an attempt to reach students who are better able to express their ideas visually than linguistically. It provides a change of pace. It also allows for a different way of conceptualizing and aids comprehension. You might connect it to the concept of the storyboard in film making, where each scene is sketched out before it is shot.

C Look for the main idea

Possible answers (page 41)

> **Main idea possibilities:** "The person solely responsible for my accomplishment and happiness was my mother." Or "... my mother is truly the guiding light of my life."

HOW IT'S WRITTEN (pages 42–43)
Examine the ending

When reading the *Writing Endings* toolbox, you may have to explain to students the idiom "run out of steam." Class discussion should lead students to see that this ending definitely fulfills the toolbox guidelines. The author uses new words, *admiration* and *gratitude*. The last line is inspirational.

TOPICS FOR WRITING (page 43)

Choose one topic to write about

For those who choose the first topic, students could decide to write about a man if they want to. "A woman/man I admire" could be a working title to be improved upon later. If students choose the second topic, refer them to the toolboxes and techniques that follow "The Model Medic" on pages 126 and 127. The third topic will provoke strong emotions. We have had colleagues who do not feel comfortable or prepared to deal with the issues raised by the topic of things students dread. Think about whether you are before giving it as an option.

AFTER WRITING (page 43)

Share your writing

Here the focus is on endings. It's also useful for students to look back at the endings of the other readings they have read so far in the book. You may need to explain the idiom "to leave someone hanging."

....

My Family Hero (pages 44–49)
Katarzyna McCarthy

This essay, written by one of our community college students about her grandmother's experience as a World War II concentration camp survivor, has an amazing story line. That story is striking for the student writer's attempts to re-create the historical period with details. May you find beginning writers like McCarthy among your students.

BEFORE READING (page 44)

Pool your knowledge

If you are using computers and whiteboards instead of chalkboards, you could let your students do some research on the Internet. If no one in the class knows what happened in these countries during World War II, that's fine. They will learn from the reading. Here are some Web sites that might be helpful: Poland and World War II: <http://www.ostrycharz.free-online.co.uk/PolishLinks.html>; Belorussia and World War II: <http://www.ecopress.org.by/english/belorussia. htm>; and Siberia: <http://www.friends-partners.org/partners/siberia/>.

AFTER READING (pages 46–47)

A Create a time line

We use time lines several times in the Student's Book when the order in which the events are told makes an essay hard to understand or when we want to give the students a way to visualize the events in the story they are reading or writing.

B Respond to the reading

Typically the response is about the cattle car, the picture of the dog, or the fact that she fell in love with a new man and had a baby while she was still in a concentration camp.

C Think about the topic

Suggest that students look back through the text and find sentences or phrases that support their answers for the first activity, the qualities that show Elizabeth to be a hero.

Possible answers (page 47)

Elizabeth: brave, courageous, clever, self-reliant, strong, a survivor, a conscientious mother, selfless

Heroes in general: (perhaps in addition to the above) leaders, role models, charismatic people; having integrity, commitment, vision; noble

HOW IT'S WRITTEN (page 48)

Think about historical references

Possible answers (page 48)

Two example sentences: "However they were captured by Russian soldiers, and in the last second Elizabeth gave them a fake name . . ." and "What I do know is that she met a young man, Joseph, who was in the Polish Armed Forces and he was also captured and became a prisoner of war."

Most students find the story frustrating in its lack of detail about World War II. It makes some students want to do research.

TOPICS FOR WRITING (page 48)

Choose one topic to write about

These three topics invite the student to write about an ordinary hero, a person who survived something, or to do some research. You will want to explain exactly what doing research involves. Here are some good starting places online: <http://www.ipl.org/div/aplus/>; and <http://www.libraryspot.com/features/paperfeature.htm>.

AFTER WRITING (page 49)

Share your writing

The sentence starters are a good way to add variety to student feedback. As always, model the activity first.

An Act of Courage (pages 49–54)

Ian Frazier

The act of courage at the heart of this excerpt takes our breath away in its action, meaning, and telling. The young woman, a Native American, comes from a different cultural history than most readers of this book, and the excerpt raises a host of issues, but most readers will feel, or hope, that they share a common humanity with her.

BEFORE READING (page 49)

A Pool your knowledge

Your students may know nothing about Native Americans in North America, or what they do know may come from the movies. You might want to give some background. Here is another helpful Web site: <http://falcon.jmu. edu/~ramseyil/native.htm>.

B Write as you read

Magic Johnson, a famous and popular U.S. professional basketball player from 1979–1992, might need explaining, as well as the notion of what it means to be five feet five and "play six foot," especially for those who think in centimeters.

AFTER READING (page 53)

A Respond to the reading

Discussing questions with a partner and then with a group before reacting can help students comprehend the story.

B Look for more information

Depending on the group, the students may have learned about the Pine Ridge Reservation, the American Indian Movement, *tiospaye*, that Indians have strict mothers, the importance of basketball to Native Americans, discrimination against Indians, how basketball games start, and that there are traditional Indian dances.

C Write a summary of the reading

The instructions here are rudimentary. Here are some useful Web sites: <http:// cwl.oregonstate.edu/h-sum.html>; <http://www.greenville.edu/faculty/dosthart/ howsumm.html>; and <http://www.uwgb.edu/esms/sss/article.htm>.

Summary writing is an important skill for academic writing. If your students are hoping to continue in academic courses, be sure to have them do this activity.

HOW IT'S WRITTEN (pages 53–54)

Appreciate action words

The first paragraph on page 52 is a good one to use: *running, dribbling, running, noise was deafening, went right down the middle, suddenly stopped, bumped, turned, tossed, stepped, unbuttoned, took it off, draped it, began to do the Lakota shawl dance, powwowin', started to sing, swaying,* etc. We're hoping that writing in their logs will encourage students to remember the importance of using strong verbs.

TOPICS FOR WRITING (page 54)

Choose one topic to write about

Another interesting approach to the first topic would be to address the issue of "it's a public service to be brave," and describe SuAnne's dance in those terms. For topic 2, refer to the Web sites indicated for doing research.

AFTER WRITING (page 54)

Share your writing

When students have written on the same topic, they may see differences and similarities more clearly than if they have written on different topics. We think reading other students' writing gives students ideas on how to revise their own piece.

HEROES: REVISION (page 55)

A Choose one piece of writing

Students may need to be encouraged not only to reread their pieces but also to read their notes about comments from classmates.

B Revise your writing

Here we suggest five steps toward revision that help to develop (add details), clarify, and focus the piece (add a title).

C Read your writing aloud

Reading your writing aloud is a technique advocated by many professional writers, as the *Writers' Tips* indicate.

D Share your writing

After students are in their circles, they could start by reading aloud the *Writers' Tips*. If needed, refer them back to the *Writing Circle* toolbox on page 20.

Believing in the True Self (pages 56–58)

Gloria Steinem

In this excerpt, Steinem raises rhetorical questions about how and why we, from babyhood on, develop or don't develop self-esteem.

BEFORE READING (page 56)

Make a personal connection

Remember as you do this activity that introspection is more valued in some Western cultures than it is in other places in the world. Some of your students may have difficulty grasping what is being asked of them here. You may want to consider demonstrating the second activity. That is, make a list of characteristics of your own true self on the whiteboard. Discuss with your students what you found easy and difficult about doing this. Did anything surprise you? What about the issue of audience? Does your true self look different if you are making your list for your students, a close friend, a colleague, or your mother?

AFTER READING (page 57)

A Understand the reading

We hope that the first activity, paraphrasing a difficult sentence, will help students better understand it and, at the same time, give them a way to work on difficult sentences. Working with a partner should aid in accuracy. The one-sentence summary activity is also done with a partner, since we believe that negotiation will usually improve understanding.

B Find deeper meanings

It may seem odd to ask students to come up with answers to questions that Steinem herself clearly states no one knows the answers to, but looking more closely at these questions can reveal what students know about individual differences – psychological, sociological, biological – as well as their particular cultural explanations for the differences described. Differences among the students' answers can generate a lively discussion.

HOW IT'S WRITTEN (page 57)

Appreciate the structure

You may find yourselves getting into a discussion of contrastive rhetoric here. Ask your students if, in their cultures, writers are encouraged to write sentences with similar patterns, using words that are the same parts of speech.

TOPICS FOR WRITING (page 58)

Choose one topic to write about

The third topic is a first step toward writing from sources as it involves interpretation and illustration of a text written by another writer.

AFTER WRITING (page 58)

Share your writing

This activity takes a good hour to complete. It is particularly important for the writer to take time to reflect on the value of a reader's feedback after an activity like this. Be sure to circulate and see that your students are taking each other's feedback seriously.

....

Becoming a Writer (pages 58–62)
Russell Baker

This autobiographical account charmingly tells a story of the author and his teacher. It contains a humorous description of the teacher and the author's recollections of his family and the process of writing a homework essay. It's an uplifting account, especially for teachers.

BEFORE READING (page 58)

Think about the topic

Students may try to tell you that there is no way on earth they can imagine what would make someone become a writer. If you meet with resistance to this task, tell them it's OK to write something silly if they can't think of anything serious. Or tell them that they are also allowed to write about what makes someone decide *not* to become a writer.

AFTER READING (page 61)

A Respond to the reading

Have your students review the *Double Entry Response* toolbox on page 26 before beginning this activity. As always, it is recommended that you do this activity yourself before assigning it to your students.

B Expand your vocabulary

We mention the dictionary here, but of course it would be better if the students could discover the meaning of the words from their context.

HOW IT'S WRITTEN (page 61)

Notice the use of repetition

At first, students may be alarmed by the repetition of the words *prim* and *primly* in paragraph 2. Point out how *specific* the detail is: *wavy hair, vested suits, collar buttons, starched white shirts, straight nose,* and so on, each one described as *prim* in some way. The repetition, each time with a new detail, helps the reader get the image Baker is trying to convey. The same is true for "don't you see."

TOPICS FOR WRITING (page 61)

The first two topics encourage the student to use Baker's piece as a model, which is very helpful for some. Those who choose the third topic will be helped by Baker's skill in describing a person.

AFTER WRITING (page 62)

Share your writing

From time to time, make sure students are giving each other feedback about the content of their writing and not correcting grammar and punctuation. It helps to remind them of Frank Smith's distinction between the author and the secretary. Loosely paraphrased, Smith says that writing involves two jobs, the author's and the secretary's. Most of the time, one person has to do both jobs. The author's job is to have the ideas, to provide details, to organize and shape ideas, and to be inspired. The secretary's job is to make sure everything is neat and correct. The trouble with schools, Smith says, is that too often we teach students to be good secretaries without ever teaching them to be good authors. Tell your students that when they meet in groups to discuss their writing, they should be meeting as a group of authors, not a group of secretaries.

....

homage to my hips (pages 62–64)
Lucille Clifton

The title says it all. Most readers will enjoy the tone of independence, pride, and I-am-what-I-am-and-don't-care-what-others-think attitude of the poem.

As of this writing, we can hear the author reading this poem at the Web site of the Academy of American Poets at <http://www.poets.org/poems/poems.cfm ?prmID=1459>.

In addition, a wonderful videotape of Clifton reading this poem and others, as well as discussing her life as a poet, is available in the series called *The Power of the Word,* narrated by Bill Moyers, produced by Public Broadcasting Service, which you may be able to find in your school or local library if you live in North America.

BEFORE READING (page 62)

A Think about the topic

Much of this unit involves raising awareness of cultural differences. If your students are from different countries, they will surprise each other with their ideas about beauty.

B Think about poetry

Sadly, most of our students almost never listen to or read poetry. No doubt students will discover, from their group discussions, that poetry is more valued in some cultures than others.

AFTER READING (page 63)

A Read and respond

As mentioned above, there is nothing better than listening to the author herself reading this poem. If you can't provide this for your students, listen to her yourself, if possible, before reading it to them. Students can be surprisingly creative and poetic in response to the activity dealing with images.

B Find deeper meanings

Awareness of the complexity underlying the surface simplicity of the poem emerges from this activity. The social issue that immediately comes to mind is slavery in the line "these hips have never been enslaved." Other issues include weight ("these hips are big hips"), pride, gender, and power.

HOW IT'S WRITTEN (pages 63–64)

Analyze the use of small letters

If you have time, compare Clifton with the twentieth-century American poet e.e. cummings (see <http://www.poets.org> under Find a Poet). Students may say that one effect of the use of small letters in this poem is to convey, in another way, the narrator's feeling of being free, not being confined by the usual "rules."

TOPICS FOR WRITING (page 64)

Choose one topic to write about

The second topic provokes much fun and laughter. An alternative is to allow students to write about someone else's body parts. One student, for instance, thrilled and surprised his classmates by writing about the beauty of his girlfriend's ear. Students who choose topic 2 need to be encouraged to focus their topic.

AFTER WRITING (page 64)

Share your writing

Be sensitive in pairing students for this activity. We want to increase awareness without increasing hostility.

. . . .

The Search for Identity (pages 64–68)

Laurence Steinberg & Ann Levine

This excerpt is more like a textbook and does not have the narrative personal flow of other readings. But in describing the adolescent's search for identity, students will find the material interesting and may reflect on their own development or compare themselves to adolescents in the United States.

BEFORE READING (pages 64–65)

A Understanding key vocabulary

We don't say how students are supposed to go about defining these words. The answer is, sometimes one of the two will know the word and explain it to the other. Otherwise they will need a dictionary. We think it's better to use an English/English dictionary, and if you're in a computer lab a good one is Merriam-Webster Online, which includes pronunciation: <http://www.m-w.com/home.htm>.

B Make predictions

The introductory information says what the excerpt is going to be about, so the question is, really, what kind of advice do you think the authors are going to give?

AFTER READING (page 66)

A Check your predictions

Making predictions before reading and then checking them for accuracy helps students focus their reading and enhance their understanding. It may encourage them to read more carefully.

B Reread and respond

This after-reading activity should be familiar to your students now.

C Explain what you read

This activity involves paraphrasing. When they get to step 3, encourage students to explain the paragraph without looking at the text or their notes if they can.

HOW IT'S WRITTEN (page 67)

Notice the use of pronouns

Because the use of nonsexist language is now a part of most style guides, it is a good idea to address it here. The place where most students say that changing the pronouns makes a difference is in the discussion of sexual awakenings because it calls very different images to mind. Steinberg and Levine avoid using *he* or *she* in several instances by using a plural noun: *teenagers, adolescents.* Reading the *Nonsexist Use of Language* toolbox will help students think of other ways to avoid gender-specific pronouns.

TOPICS FOR WRITING (page 68)

Choose one topic to write about

In Japan, where one of us is teaching, the first topic evoked bitter invectives about the entrance examination system in Japanese higher education. Still, it was more popular, perhaps because less personal, than topic 2 or 3.

AFTER WRITING (page 68)

Share your writing

Be sure students use the *Reader's Response Feedback* toolbox on page 15 as a guide for their feedback.

. . . .

Smoking (pages 68–71)
Judith Rich Harris

This piece is about preventing teenagers from smoking. It has a teenage quality to the writing, lively, slangy, and fast-moving. And it's as much about teenagers as it is about smoking. We've found our students love to write about smoking, perhaps because they have the essay already written in their heads. This piece may challenge them by its focus and style to say something different this time. Prepare them for the reading.

BEFORE READING (page 68)

A Think about the topic

Depending on where you live, students may not be willing to admit that they smoke or even know people who smoke.

B Write as you read

Technically, this is a "while reading" activity rather than a "before reading" activity. You might mention to the students that they will be stopping three times to write.

AFTER READING (page 70)

A Share your responses

Make sure the students review the *Main Idea* toolbox on page 35, before embarking on this activity.

B Understand the reading

The author's writing style may not be easy for students to understand, as it is somewhat casual and "teen" sounding. Students will no doubt have many questions about words, expressions, sentences, or paragraphs they didn't understand. Class discussion will probably be important for helping them satisfactorily comprehend the reading.

C Find the main ideas

The discussions in activity B above and working with a partner should help students write fairly accurate main point sentences.

HOW IT'S WRITTEN (pages 70–71)

A Notice the use of pronouns

Harris has made the choice to use *she* as her singular pronoun, possibly because of the recent rise in smoking among teenaged girls. Students should notice a marked difference in the use of pronouns in "The Search for Identity" (pages 65–66) where the authors always use *he* as the singular pronoun. (You might want to refer to the *Nonsexist Use of Language* toolbox on page 67.)

B Think about the writing style

The author uses the language of the group she is talking about, which helps readers empathize with what she is saying if they know teenagers.

TOPICS FOR WRITING (page 71)

Choose a topic to write about

Note that we encourage students to use pre-writing techniques to gather ideas. We almost always do this in our classes. Please follow this practice yourself, even when the book doesn't specifically suggest it! The third topic is another case of offering the student the excerpt as a model for an essay. Some students are particularly grateful for this kind of guidance. Others would rather strike out on their own.

AFTER WRITING (page 71)

Share your writing

Hearing what others have written about the topic they chose may give students ideas for expansion of their own writing.

IDENTITY: REVISION (pages 72–73)

A Choose one piece of writing

This time students are asked to choose two pieces initially and then get suggestions from a partner as to which piece has more potential for revision.

B Use the ARMS method to revise

In this revision section, we introduce the technique known by the acronym ARMS (Add, Remove, Move, Substitute). We find that these guidelines enable students to give each other specific advice in concrete ways, as well as give them a way to look at their own writing more objectively. When we introduce the concept of ARMS, we often ask students to write for 15 minutes or so on an unrelated topic, and then we go through each step of ARMS with them one by one, so they clearly see what we mean when we say *add, remove, move,* and *substitute*. This activity can take up to an hour or so, but it's well worth it. It also helps to show students a paper that is marked up in ways suggested, complete with arrows, additions (perhaps even using scissors and tape to cut and add), cross-outs, and so on. You might use a first draft of your own writing or a paper from a student in another class. Students really see that going through the steps of ARMS and marking up a paper can have value for revising, even if they have used a computer for their initial writing. Your students may come back and thank you for teaching them ARMS.

C Share your writing

This sharing technique is somewhat different from others we have used so far. Readers have some leeway in what they say to a writer, and writers will have at least three different responses to their work.

New Vistas and Ventures

UNIT PREVIEW (pages 76–77)

A Make connections

At the beginning of this unit, we encourage students to make connections between the title of the unit and Helen Nearing's "When one door closes, another opens." If you think students will not know the meanings of *vista* and *venture*, you will want to clarify these words before they begin the freewriting.

B Make a personal connection

The life map connection works well. Sometimes giving an example from your own life helps. In fact, for all of the activities in **Inspired *to* Write**, it's a good idea to do them by yourself, or better yet, with a colleague, before presenting them to your class, so that you come to class with your own examples ready in case students are stumped by a prompt.

C Respond to quotes

These quotations about change may call up some traumatic experiences.

D Preview Unit 2

A quick look through this unit may bring up some of the following connections: beginnings, arrivals, leavings; weddings, courtship; first job, career choices; hope, success, grief, crying, laughing, and accidents.

Opening New Doors

The First Day (pages 78–82)
Edward P. Jones

Your students may be interested in knowing that in 2004, Jones won a Pulitzer prize for his novel *A Known World*. This excerpt, however, is part of a short story. It depicts a child's first day at school in a way that tells as much about the mother and the school officials as about the child.

BEFORE READING (page 78)

Gather ideas about the topic

Review the *Clustering* toolbox on page 12.

AFTER READING (page 80)

A Respond to the reading

The response questions are intentionally open-ended. Please remind your students that there are no wrong answers.

B List important events

Possible answers (page 80)

> **Important events:** an hour on her hair; entering the crowded auditorium, seeing the new school, seeing the woman with dollar bills in her hair; learning that her mother can't read, the separation, and the sound of her mother's footsteps.

HOW IT'S WRITTEN (pages 80–81)

A Label emotions

There are the narrator's emotions and the mother's. Students will see that they are mostly negative. Some of the names of the emotions include fear, anticipation, anxiety, doubt, sorrow, confusion, competitiveness, possessiveness, and curiosity.

B Learn about showing

This is an important lesson for writers. Here are three places where the author shows instead of tells the emotion:

> *"The woman looks up slowly as if she has heard this question once too often."*

> *"My mother looks at me, then looks away. I know almost all of her looks, but this one is brand new to me."*

> *"Her lips are quivering."*

In the *Writer's Tip*, Natalie Goldberg answers the question about why showing is effective. Another good example of emotions that are shown instead of told is in the next reading, "A Walk to the Jetty."

TOPICS FOR WRITING (page 81)

Choose one topic to write about

Emphasize the importance of showing, not telling, in all three topics. The third topic doesn't have to be about a parent. It could also be about some other person the writer admired or idolized.

AFTER WRITING (page 82)

Share your writing

The *Asking for Feedback* toolbox demonstrates another technique that works best if it is modeled. This time, try using a piece of your own writing. The students will be amazed that you are seriously asking them for their help, but if you are serious, they will be too, and you will get some good advice from them. Another option is to use a piece of student writing from a previous term. If you are working in a computer lab, the feedback can be done electronically.

....

A Walk to the Jetty (pages 82–87)
Jamaica Kincaid

This piece is a favorite from previous editions of this book, in large part because it displays such colorful, descriptive writing about a topic that students identify with.

BEFORE READING (pages 82–83)

A Make a list

The list does not have to be only about traumatic, heart-rending situations. It can also be leaving and going back, for instance, leaving home to go to school, leaving school to go on vacation, and so on. For activity 3, students could be encouraged to *show* their feelings rather than tell. (See the *Show – Don't Tell* toolbox on page 81.)

B Locate the setting

If you have a large wall map, have student partners show the class the locations.

AFTER READING (page 85)

A Read and respond

If this is the first time your students are doing a double entry response, be sure to go over the technique with them. (See the *Double Entry Response* toolbox on page 26.)

B Make a visual representation

You may want to refer back to the notes in the Teacher's Manual on page 17 and to pages 41–42 in the Student's Book.

C Learn words through context

This is a new activity. Sometimes students resist the effort involved and try to sneak out their bilingual dictionaries! Some words our students have circled include *hollow, anchored, stevedores, shriveled, bobbed, scorn, stupor,* and *swallowed.*

HOW IT'S WRITTEN (page 86)

Appreciate descriptive language

Finding the colors and sounds is a relatively easy task, but metaphors and similes take more time. Our examples help students get started. Be patient as they work through this task.

Possible answers (page 86)

> **Some metaphors and similes:** I felt I was being held down against my will. I felt I was burning up from head to toe. I felt that someone was tearing me up into little pieces; the words "I shall never see this again" spilled out inside me; bobbed up and down inside me; as if a vessel filled with liquid had been placed on its side and now was slowly emptying out.

TOPICS FOR WRITING (pages 86–87)

Choose one topic to write about

If students write about leaving in topic 1, then when writing about topic 2 they should use an experience other than leaving. As for topic 3, Kincaid provides many provocative starting places, such as "I felt I was being held down against my will."

AFTER WRITING (page 87)

Share your writing

If students are having difficulty with titles, suggest they look at the *Titles* toolbox on page 38.

· ·

On Turning Fifty (pages 87–91)
Judy Scales-Trent

Your students may not be near the age of 50, but they can appreciate the feelings of a person approaching an important milestone in life.

BEFORE READING (page 87)

Think about the topic

Two of the topics for writing relate to this freewriting, so that when students have done it, they are on their way to writing an essay. Number 2 says "unless it is too private." This is one of the ground rules for our classes. No one is forced to share. Everyone can choose to be silent.

AFTER READING (pages 89–90)

A Respond to the reading

A triple entry response is a double entry response with one more response. If your students are starting to get comfortable with sharing their writing together, they generally enjoy this and sometimes become competitive. As a variation, you can write the third entry.

B Label emotions

Possible answers (page 90)

> **Some emotions students wrote in the margins:** disappointment, regret, surprise, loneliness, sadness, longing, peace, wholeness, fear, dread, satisfaction, and ambivalence.

HOW IT'S WRITTEN (page 90)

Appreciate the structure

Scales-Trent compares herself to her mother, her sisters, her new colleague, and her mother again, at first seeing differences between her life and her mother's, then similarities. The essay is neatly organized, but the significance in the order is open to interpretation. Her discoveries include that something went wrong, the morning in Buffalo when she saw how her life could be right, a sense of peace, planting bulbs, and similarity with her mother after all.

TOPICS FOR WRITING (page 90)

Choose one topic to write about

All three topics encourage students to reflect on their lives. Our students have found these topics appealing.

AFTER WRITING (page 91)

A Read your writing aloud

Although your students may be familiar with reading their writing aloud (see the *Reading Aloud* toolbox on page 55), writing down emotions they felt and those they wanted to express is a new activity. You may need to talk about this step. Students may also want to show, not tell, about the emotions they felt as they read their writing aloud and ask themselves if their expressions succeeded.

B Share your writing

Again, make sure students understand what to do.

The Transitions of Life (pages 91–96)

Carole Wade & Carol Tavris

This reading is a move toward something more academic.

BEFORE READING (page 91)

A Gather ideas about the topic

Milestones that students come up with include birth, starting school, making a friend, joining a team, graduating from high school, getting married, and getting a job. You may need to give them some examples of a person who doesn't reach one of the milestones at the "expected" age, say, someone who does not have a full-time job and/or is not married at 40.

B Write as you read

Check to make sure that students stop and write after each section. The writing, however, will be brief.

AFTER READING (pages 94–95)

A Share your responses

Here are some examples of what our students learned: what affects people most is not whether what they do is expected or unexpected when they do it; that people who cannot do things "on time" may feel depressed and anxious; that midlife is typically a time of psychological well-being, good health, productivity, and community involvement.

B Compare cultures

You might check with your colleagues about their ideas, but we wrote down that the "right" ages in the United States are: moving out after high school or after college, 18–23; getting married, 25; having children, 25–39; empty nest, 50–55; becoming a grandparent, 55–65; retirement, 65; old age, 80. Myths include that midlife is a time of turmoil; that American women in their 50s are happy (see previous reading).

HOW IT'S WRITTEN (page 95)

Learn about using references

Here we introduce citations, an important part of academic writing. A great deal of instruction about how and why to use citations is available online. Here are just a couple of sites: <http://www.dianahacker.com/resdoc/>; and <http://owl.english.purdue.edu/>.

After reading about citations and answering the questions, it seems to us that the most important question to answer is number 3.

TOPICS FOR WRITING (page 96)

Choose one topic to write about

Each of these topics encourages students to apply what they have just learned about citing sources.

AFTER WRITING (page 96)

Share your writing

Be sure students use the *Sentence Starter Feedback* toolbox on page 49 as a guide for giving their feedback. They can give feedback either orally or in writing, as you wish.

OPENING NEW DOORS: REVISION (pages 97–98)

A Choose one piece of writing

This activity can be done in class or assigned for homework.

B Revise your writing

Remember to refer students to the *Titles* toolbox on page 38.

C Proofread

This technique may seem boring and pointless for students who are used to working on computers with spelling and grammar checkers, but here is a small sample of the kinds of errors we found in the manuscript of our book that those devices did not catch: *dong* for *doing,* "mom would get made [mad] at me," "who now words [works] as a sign-language interpreter." Enough said.

D Share your writing

See notes about writing circles in the Teacher's Manual on page 9. Encourage students to reread the *Writing Circle* toolbox on page 20.

E Reflect on writing techniques

This is often difficult for students to do, so a whole-class discussion about the techniques and their values may be useful.

Dating and Marriage

Pebbles (pages 99–101)
lê thi diem thúy

Ah, romance. This excerpt is like a poem, a close-up in words.

BEFORE READING (page 99)

Gather ideas about the topic

In some cultures, dating is not a familiar concept. In that case, tell students they can freewrite instead about how decisions about marriage were made in the past or how their grandparents or parents met. For number 3, our students have come up with the following: eye contact, smiling, winking, standing close, touching a hand, shoulder, or knee.

AFTER READING (pages 99–100)

A Respond to the reading

See the *Ways to Read Poetry* toolbox on page 62.

B Make a personal connection

Students may draw on and further develop the material they were working on in *Before Reading*. If you are working with a homogeneous group, ask some of them to write about what they have heard about other cultures.

HOW IT'S WRITTEN (page 100)

Appreciate poetic language

Possible answers (page 100)

> **Phrases students underlined:** in anger, in desperation, in joy; touched her like warm kisses; Warm kisses on the curve of her back, sliding down the crook of her arm, grazing her ankles and landing around her feet in the hot sand.

Remind your students of "Becoming a Writer" (pages 59–60) and "A Walk to the Jetty" (pages 83–84) where there were also numerous repetitions. This excerpt also has similes and metaphors that students might notice.

TOPICS FOR WRITING (page 100)

Choose one topic to write about

For topic 1, students may look back at the *Using Your Senses* toolbox on page 10. Topics 2 and 3 are similar, but topic 2 is focused on love. Also, topic 2 could more easily be turned into an academic essay.

AFTER WRITING (page 101)

Share your writing

In this activity, we are picturing the classroom as an art gallery through which students wander and admire each other's work. It might be wise to discuss what makes an essay effective before sending students off to take notes.

Kids Talk about Dating across Cultural Lines

(pages 101–105)

These excerpts are from interviews of kids and, thus, have a spoken English flavor and quality. There's a realness to them, and our students have enjoyed reading them.

BEFORE READING (page 101)

Gather ideas about the topic

You may have to explain the concept of dating. If students don't know the positives and negatives of dating someone from another culture, they may have to imagine them. You could tell them, in number 3, to think of the qualities they think are important in someone they would like to go to the movies with or to their favorite place with.

AFTER READING (pages 104–105)

A Respond to the reading

One student chose to respond to this statement: "And I guess I'm proud of my Puerto Rican culture, and I'd like my child to be just as proud, and not to have to worry about that."

B Find issues

Refer to Kenneth Bruffee's inspiring book A Short Course in Writing for more details about issues and generalizations.

Possible answers (pages 104–105)

Issues: dating outside one's race; deceiving our parents (friend instead of boyfriend); mother's and father's different perceptions of dating; cultural pride; cultural stereotyping.

Questions: Is there ever a time when it's appropriate to deceive our parents? Is it right to deceive our parents? Is it wrong to deceive our parents?

Generalization: There are times when it is necessary to deceive our parents.

Opposing generalization: It is never appropriate to deceive our parents.

Support: If our parents don't understand the culture we are living in . . .
If our parents are bigots, racists, homophobes, etc.
If our parents are alcoholics or drug addicts.
If our parents don't love us.

HOW IT'S WRITTEN (page 105)

Recognize spoken and written English

Help students recognize the difference between spoken and written English. One example is the preponderance of *like* or *I guess*. Or the phrase ". . . just the fact that he's not Puerto Rican, period" (saying the punctuation aloud).

TOPICS FOR WRITING (page 105)

Choose one topic to write about

You might want to discuss with students how they like to spend their free time and with whom and why before they write about the perfect date. Your students may or may not be at a level of proficiency that they can write "spoken" English. Another idea for topic 3 would be to have the students find a partner and interview each other.

AFTER WRITING (page 105)

Share your writing

Students tend to pass the honors around, and over time a class will hear from many different voices if left to student choice.

....

Weddings (pages 106–110)

Fauziya Kassindja and Layli Miller Bashir

This excerpt of a family member's wedding in Togo, West Africa, captures in great detail the rituals and practices of a marriage ceremony, which may not be altogether different from other wedding traditions but is certainly among the most celebratory.

BEFORE READING (page 106)

A Ask questions

Many students were struck by the sharp contrast between the facts about the author and the topic of her writing. Did she envy her sister, they wondered? Is she married now? Did she fall in love? Did her sister?

B Locate the setting

Knowledge about Togo, Benin, or Nigeria from a student who has been there might be shared with the class.

C Write as you read

Once again, check to make sure that students stop and write after each section. The writing, however, will be brief.

AFTER READING (pages 108–109)

A Share responses

Students can share orally, especially if they've written just notes for themselves, or they can pass their writing to their partner. Students are kept on their toes if you vary the way they share.

Dating and Marriage   **39**

B Compare cultures

Charts are often used in the Student's Book to help students organize information they have read. Students could divide this chart into stages, too, if they like.

Possible answers (page 108)

Cultural Practices in Togo	Cultural Practices in My Culture
Dating Parents play a big role in choosing the partner.	Dating Parents are sometimes the last to know.
The Engagement Period The young man visits the woman only after the wedding date is set.	The Engagement Period Couples spend a lot of time together without even thinking about marriage.
The Wedding Ceremony Family members, like aunts and uncles, gather several weeks before to prepare.	The Wedding Ceremony Extended family members come for just a day or two.

Students discover that different practices help different people in different ways.

HOW IT'S WRITTEN (page 109)

Identify general and specific information

In a nutshell, there are a lot more general statements at the beginning of the essay. Specific statements fall just before and after the first break and again after the second and third breaks.

TOPICS FOR WRITING (page 109)

Choose one topic to write about

If students choose the second topic, they can be referred to the *Interview Tips* toolbox as well as the *Writer's Tip,* both on page 127.

AFTER WRITING (page 110)

Share your writing

For some teachers in this age of information technology, attaching a piece of paper may seem old-fashioned and out of date. Please use whatever techniques are available, including e-mail, Microsoft Word Track Changes, and so on.

DATING AND MARRIAGE: REVISION (pages 111–112)

A Choose one piece of writing

If there's time, have students discuss why they made the choices they did. Sometimes they choose the piece that seems most finished. Sometimes it's the ideas in the piece they want to develop.

B Revise your writing

The advice on revision in the *Revision Tips* toolbox from Meredith Sue Willis is useful. Remind the students about the *Titles* toolbox on page 38.

C Share your writing

This, too, could be done via e-mail if it's available to your students.

Work

The First Job (pages 113–115)

Sandra Cisneros

This story describes a young girl's first day on her first job, which is typical of first days, full of her awareness of job details and feelings, but this first day ends with a shock: her first experience of sexual harassment on the job.

BEFORE READING (page 113)

Think about the topic

This pre-reading activity is fun for students as long as everyone has had a job, but provokes guilt in those who haven't and are being supported by others. Suggest that they could also talk about first jobs friends and family have had.

AFTER READING (page 114)

A Respond to the reading

Students will discover, some to their dismay, that this reading is not really about work at all, but about the loss of innocence (because of the last paragraph).

B Make a visual representation

By asking students to draw the story in four pictures and then add another paragraph and another picture, we give them an opportunity to deal with the shock of the story's ending.

HOW IT'S WRITTEN (page 115)

Examine the ending

Here the focus is on the shock value of the switch to the present tense, giving the awful moment more immediacy and also making it more like spoken language. Her telling it this way also reminds us of her youth.

TOPICS FOR WRITING (page 115)

Choose one topic to write about

In topic 1, we do not mean to imply that Cisneros's incident was included to show what the job was like for her. For topic 2, you may need to explain the expression "being taken advantage of." It will be interesting to ask students who wrote about topic 3 to talk about it when you discuss the next excerpt, "Behind the Counter," on page 116.

AFTER WRITING (page 115)

Share your writing

We suggest you briefly review these toolboxes on feedback with students to remind them of their choices.

. . . .

Behind the Counter (pages 116–120)

Eric Schlosser

This excerpt discusses the exploitation of teenagers by the fast food industry. The writer interviewed kids and presents their stories and words to support his points about the cycle of exploitation and cheap, compliant labor.

BEFORE READING (page 116)

Test your knowledge

This is a pre-reading activity with an edge: a quiz before you've read the material.

AFTER READING (pages 118–119)

A Check your answers

Students often guess incorrectly about numbers 3, 4, and 7.

B Annotate the reading

Annotation is an acquired skill that takes time and practice to develop. Some students have been trained not to make any marks in a book and will have a hard time overcoming this training. Please annotate the text yourself first and show them, boldly, how it is done. If students plan to sell their textbooks, they could work with a photocopy.

C Find advantages and disadvantages

Possible answers (page 119)

One student wrote this:

Advantages	Disadvantages
1 Managers can pay low wages to teenagers.	1 Need to wake up early in the morning.
2 Managers can come in late sometimes.	2 Difficult to stand a long time.
3 Few working hours (e.g., 20 hours a week) may, like work experience, gain an increased sense of personal success.	3 They need to open the shop in the morning and close it at night every day.
4 They feel happy when they get the money.	4 Longer working hours (more than 20 hours a week) will be a risk to teenager's future educational and financial success.
	5 Boys can commit petty crime . . .
	6 Sometimes they face rude attitude from the customers.
	7 Teenagers don't like their work.

HOW IT'S WRITTEN (page 119)

Identify general and specific information

Students will quickly realize the skillful way in which the author alternates general statements with specific examples.

Possible answers (page 119)

For number 3, one student wrote: The story describes the general conditions of teenagers' part-time jobs. It can be said that teenagers are bound to do the jobs to continue to study and live. When they start, they enjoy the work. But gradually they hate the jobs and often change their place of work. After doing the work a few months, they want to earn more money, and they stop going to school and also commit some crimes.

The character of Elisa describes how exceptional some teenagers are. By reading the story, teenagers can have inspiration to change themselves as Elisa is doing.

TOPICS FOR WRITING (page 120)

Choose one topic to write about

These topics, which ask for facts and examples, cry out for "gathering ideas" before you write: freewriting (page 2), brainstorming a list (page 7), clustering (page 12), and creating a Venn diagram (page 131) are techniques used to help gather ideas. Remind students of these useful techniques and that they can employ any of them at any point in the writing/drafting process.

AFTER WRITING (page 120)

Share your writing

Rather than write directly on someone else's paper, students might like the idea of using a separate piece. It seems respectful. They might like it if you do it on their writing, as well.

To be of use (pages 120–123)
Marge Piercy

In this poem, Piercy gives us a metaphorical view of hard work. You can listen to Piercy read her work at: <http://www.cortlandreview.com/issue/10/piercy10.htm> or read all about her at the Marge Piercy homepage: <http://www.archer-books.com/Piercy/>.

BEFORE READING (page 120)
Think about the topic
Students have written that they thought scientists, doctors, teachers, and artists, among others, did significant, important, and meaningful work.

AFTER READING (pages 121–122)
A Read and respond
In our opinion, poetry is meant to be read aloud because it is so rich, condensed, and packed with meaning, sounds, and images. Reading aloud is a way to appreciate this and a way to slow down.

B Make a personal connection
Most of the time, Piercy's description is very different from the students'. Remind them that this does not mean that theirs is bad or wrong.

C Act out the poem
A group of high school teachers taking a course in literacy at Lesley University in Mount Vernon, Washington, gave us the idea for this activity, and we thank them for it.

HOW IT'S WRITTEN (page 122)
A Find metaphors and similes
There are almost no lines in this poem that do not contain a metaphor or simile, with the animals – seals, ox, water buffalo – coming first.

B Listen to the sounds
Again, we ask students to listen. Obviously some will appreciate this more than others.

Possible answers (page 122)

> **Alliteration:** sleek heads of seals, bouncing like half-submerged balls, mud and muck, who do what has to be done, the work of the world, worth doing well done, a shape that satisfies

TOPICS FOR WRITING (page 123)

Choose one topic to write about

Students choosing topic 1 might feel that Piercy has said all there is to say about the work of the world and request permission to write a poem about something else. Please grant it. Topic 2 encourages the beginning of a response to literature. For advice on this kind of writing, send students to Purdue University's Online Writing Lab: <http://owl.english.purdue.edu/>.

AFTER WRITING (page 123)

Share your writing

It never hurts to hear positive things about your writing or to have your students walk out of class with smiles on their faces. The results are positively motivating. When students write in the atmosphere of positive comments, they'll never stop.

....

The Model Medic (pages 123–128)
Sarah Freeman

The writer gives us a newspaper profile of a woman who chooses a career as a paramedic over fashion modeling. The writer/reporter interviewed her subjects.

BEFORE READING (page 123)

Think about the topic

Some students don't recognize the vocabulary *model, medic,* or *paramedic,* although they know what these jobs are. It helps to bring in a two- or three-minute video clip of a model and of a medic. Both are relatively easy to find, particularly the latter with the worldwide popularity of the American television program *ER*.

This profile contains quite a bit of difficult language, including language that it is unpleasant to explain (the first sentence, for instance). Prepare in advance!

AFTER READING (pages 125–126)

A Respond to the reading

This is an opportunity to review some of the responses to reading that have been covered previously and to give students a chance to express their preferences.

B Find positive and negative points

Possible answers (page 126)

Occupation	Positive Points	Negative Points
Model	• A "life of glamour and privilege" • Modeling took her to New York City • Travel abroad (Paris, Milan)	• Vulnerable as young girls • Exploited by the agencies • Modeling doesn't last for long
Paramedic	• Enjoyable and challenging work • Close relationships with colleagues • Opportunity to help people	• Sometimes the job is dangerous • People may get angry or even violent because of fear • Hectic and stressful

HOW IT'S WRITTEN (page 126)

Discover how writers use questions

The Reporter's Formula toolbox is useful for many different kinds of writing, and as students go back over the piece, they will notice that Freeman made use of all of these questions. For number 3, most students wished they could see a picture of Rhona Chambers working as a model and then as a paramedic. We couldn't find one, but maybe you can find one that works.

TOPICS FOR WRITING (page 127)

Choose one topic to write about

The topics for writing are all interviews, and the instructions contain lots of tips about how to do interviews. If you are living in a country where there are no English speakers available to be interviewed, students can do this assignment via e-mail. For one class, one of the authors of this book recruited about 30 of her friends who had interesting jobs or knew someone who did. For another, she had students do a search at <http://www.bls.gov/oes/home.htm> for descriptions of jobs they wanted to know about. Then she had them search the Internet for people who were doing the jobs they were interested in learning about. Students then wrote to a stranger, explaining the assignment and asking if they could interview the person. Nine times out of ten they received a positive reply. The results were very exciting. For some of the students, it was the first time they had communicated with a native speaker of English other than a teacher. At the end of the term, they all mentioned this assignment as their most positive experience with English to date.

AFTER WRITING (pages 127–128)

Share your writing

This activity, too, can buzz with excitement if students are actually meeting people and talking to them, live or online.

WORK: REVISION (pages 129–130)

A Choose one piece of writing

This revision section focuses on beginnings. The rereading and discussion of beginnings is an important part of the work, although two of the four readings in this subsection are not the beginning of the piece of writing. Have students also look at the beginning of "Brothers" (page 4), "Safe" (page 22), "No Comprendo" (page 34), "The First Day" (page 78), and "On Turning Fifty" (page 87).

B Improve the beginning

Students may resist the suggestion in number 4 to write three different beginnings. Do it with them to show them how it is done.

C Share your writing

You might have students finish up by writing a reflection on how they wrote and revised the piece, what was easy, what was hard, what part they like best, and what they think of their beginning.

Exploring Emotions

Hope Emerges As Key to Success in Life
(pages 131–136)

Daniel Goleman

This kind of text would be found in the self-help section of psychology books, very popular in the United States. This happens to draw on research about students and might give some hope and help to students in your class.

BEFORE READING (page 131)

A Gather ideas about the topic

If you're not familiar with Venn diagrams and you want more information, and perhaps guidance, go to <http://www.google.com> and search "Venn diagrams." You'll find sites for teachers (you may have to register). Some include other "graphic organizers," which are used with students for comprehending readings, getting ideas and themes for writing, or learning concepts in any course.

In this exercise, our students struggled with the introduction of the Venn diagram and having to make one themselves about hope and success. Show them one already done first. See <http://www.venndiagram.com/> or, as suggested above, use a search engine like Google to find "graphic organizers." Let students refer to an example as they work.

B Write as you read

Some of your students may think this is one of our favorite forms of torture. Remind them that good readers read with pen in hand. They mark up the text, write questions and comments, agree, disagree, etc., and, in so doing, write their own text.

AFTER READING (pages 133–134)

A Respond to the reading

Students could also add to their Venn diagrams.

B Understand the reading

Possible answers (page 134)

> **One student restated the bulleted points as follows:**
>
> **1** People with hope ask their friends for help; people without it don't.
>
> **2** People with hope are like Susan B. Anthony saying, "Failure is impossible."
>
> **3** When they are in trouble, they look on the bright side and say, "This too shall pass."
>
> **4** If getting up at six in the morning doesn't work, they stay up until midnight to finish what they have to do.
>
> **5** If their grades in chemistry and physics aren't good enough to go to medical school, they think about becoming a paramedic.
>
> **6** They do their work one step at a time, making it as easy as possible so they don't get frustrated.

HOW IT'S WRITTEN (pages 134–135)

A Think about headings

Headings are signposts to tell the reader what direction the piece will go in next.

B Observe references to experts

This instruction on references to experts is to help the students learn about how academic writing works. Do the exercises yourself first so you can talk about them clearly. This section leads to the *Quoting and Paraphrasing* toolbox, which we will refer to many times in the next unit.

TOPICS FOR WRITING (page 135)

Choose one topic to write about

Learning to cite articles, including Web sources, and to summarize articles are essential to success in school. If you ask instructors across the curriculum what they want students to be able to do, they will name these two things at the top of their lists.

AFTER WRITING (page 136)

Share your writing

It is probably time to model the process for the class again. Ask one group of students to come to the front of the room and model for the others.

. . . .

It's O.K. to Cry: Tears Are Not Just a Bid for Attention (pages 136–140)

Jane Brody

Note about the reading: Because this reading is dated, we deleted a reference to Edmund Muskie's crying in public that began the article, but students complained about how difficult it was to read because there seemed to be no beginning. We were glad they had learned this lesson about beginnings, but sorry we deprived them of one for this piece. Here is the original first paragraph:

> Crying is hardly an activity encouraged by society. Tears, be they of sorrow, anger, or joy, typically make Americans feel uncomfortable and embarrassed. Edmund S. Muskie may well have lost his bid for the 1972 Presidential candidacy when he wept while denouncing a newspaper publisher for printing a letter that insulted his wife.

Since the article was published, new research indicates that people may not be "the only animals definitely known to shed emotional tears." See, for instance, *When Elephants Weep: The Emotional Lives of Animals* by Susan McCarthy and Jeffrey Moussaieff Masson (Delta: 1996).

BEFORE READING (page 136)

Think about the topic

Privately, in their freewriting, most students in one class admitted that they cried often. In the group and whole class discussions, however, they did not make the same admission.

AFTER READING (page 139)

A Respond to the reading

Most students we worked with were amazed at the multiple benefits of tears and could easily complete this activity.

B Observe references to experts

Our students found and understood Brody's references to the experts in part B. We emphasized two points here: One is that academic writing uses references because it is writing by scholars for scholars, and the other is that if a person is writing about a scientific topic and is not a scientist herself, she needs to cite the research of scientists to support her claims.

HOW IT'S WRITTEN (page 139)

A Examine the beginning

Again, students said the introduction was not effective. They are correct. It is not really the introduction of the piece.

B Notice how research is reported

Possible answers (page 139)

> **Words and expressions used to report research:** "although some researchers have suggested . . ."; "the new studies suggest . . ."; "University of Minnesota researchers who are studying the chemical composition of tears have recently isolated . . ."; "Researchers at several other institutions are investigating . . ."; and so on.

TOPICS FOR WRITING (pages 139–140)

Choose one topic to write about

Topic 1 invites a paraphrase of the research Brody reports, as does topic 2. In order to accomplish what is required in topic 3, please refer the students to the handouts available.

AFTER WRITING (page 140)

Share your writing

Proofreading this way (also called "editing aloud") helps students use their ears and eyes to refine and check their writing. We use it ourselves all the time. Encourage it as a habit for your students.

· ·

Going Through the House (pages 140–144)
Claire Braz-Valentine

This strong, humorous poem is a favorite of some instructors who've used it; it has universal appeal. Braz-Valentine has a Web site where you can hear her read another poem: <http://homepage.mac.com/clairebraz/>.

BEFORE READING (page 140)

Think about the topic

This poem contains some language that some students will find shocking, others useful. A recently divorced student was delighted to learn the phrase "your smug scumsucking voice." Please note: Both the topic and the poem call up strong emotions. Remember to give the students the right to pass on sharing their freewriting.

AFTER READING (pages 142–143)

A Read and respond

Depending on the level of students you are teaching and their familiarity with slang, one initial reaction to the poem might be bewilderment. We have found it advisable to have ready definitions for such terms as "smart ass," "wise ass grin," "Who gives a shit?" and "scumsucking voice," so as not to be caught off guard.

B Analyze the author's feelings

Students usually understand that she cares very much.

HOW IT'S WRITTEN (page 143)

A Notice specific details

The list is long and opinions differ about what makes her the angriest, but many students think it's the greeting cards that talk about love forever.

B Study the verbs

The verbs are powerful and will add greatly to the students' repertoire. Some of the verbs voted most powerful were *yank, smash, shred, rip,* and *pulverize.*

TOPICS FOR WRITING (pages 143–144)

Choose one topic to write about

If the first two topics are too threatening, suggest that the students choose topic 3 and write about someone else.

AFTER WRITING (page 144)

A Make your verbs effective
B Make your images effective

We included the revision activities in A and B before students share their writing. They could be done at home.

C Share your writing

You may want to have a group model this activity.

....

Black Steer Canyon (pages 145–148)
Terry Tempest Williams

The author's experience of hiking and getting injured and scarred, as well as her interpretation, take readers to places they've never been before.

BEFORE READING (page 145)

Relate to the setting

It helps students understand exactly what happens in this story if they can picture it geographically. If there is time, students could make a senses list as they did in the *Using Your Senses* toolbox on page 10.

AFTER READING (page 147)

A Find the main events

Possible answers (page 147)

> **Underlined events:** (they) descended into Black Steer Canyon; lost my footing . . . tumbled down the cliff; yelled to see if I was all right; pressure wound on my forehead . . . popped open; medical technician . . . was trying to stop the bleeding; I relaxed; I (had to) carry me out; Brooke and I climbed out of the canyon . . . traversed the desert; arrived in Salt Lake City . . . surgeon reopened the cut; I have been marked by the desert; to enter wilderness is to court risk; landscapes we know become places of solace; I will return to Dark Canyon; unknown Utah . . . is a landscape of the imagination; many native cultures participate in scarification rituals; I looked in the mirror . . . saw a red scar

B Respond to the reading

This task should now be familiar to your students and done with relative ease.

C Understand the lessons learned

This activity leads up to the *How It's Written* activity. Students may want to expand their ideas of ways they can end a piece of writing.

HOW IT'S WRITTEN (page 148)

Examine the ending

Obviously, we think the ending begins rather early in this piece. Some students agree that the ending begins with the line "I have been marked by the desert."

This is certainly a major turning point in the essay. Others insist that it begins with "It's no secret . . ." The choice is yours.

TOPICS FOR WRITING (page 148)

Choose one topic to write about

Topics 1 and 2 could be combined.

AFTER WRITING (page 148)

Share your writing

This is our basic format for sharing and getting feedback.

EXPLORING EMOTIONS: REVISION (pages 149–150)

A Choose one piece of writing

Given that the focus of this revision is adding information to essays, you may want to suggest that students look for pieces that have the most potential for expansion.

B Add to your writing

The *Adding Information to Essays* toolbox nudges students toward taking a scholarly approach to writing. If you haven't already done so, this would be a good time to arrange for them to have a tour of the school library and its resources. Depending on your situation, reference librarians are usually more than happy to help students learn about what is available to them in the library and online.

C Get feedback

Perhaps you found this form and used it before. It fits this revision well. You might adapt it to suit other revision work.

D Share your writing

This is an alternative form of publishing. If the class has a bulletin board, post copies of a selection (with students' help and agreement) for students in other classes to see, or make a publication.

UNIT 3

A Changing World

UNIT PREVIEW (pages 152–153)

A Make connections

Bartoe was in outer space. He flew on a space shuttle in 1985 and wrote these words about what he saw. If you can find a copy of *The Home Planet*, edited by Kevin W. Kelley, you can show students some of the 150 stunning photographs taken by astronauts from outer space. Students may also be interested in reading some of the other impressions and recollections of the astronauts from many different countries quoted in this book. As Kelley says, "Space offers us a chance to see our world with new eyes, a perspective that may have great significance for the planet for all of the future."

B Gather ideas about the topic

Here we introduce the concept of looping, invented by Peter Elbow in his book *Writing with Power*.

Possible answers (page 153)

> **Three loops written by one student:**
>
> A Changing World
>
> 1) One thing I noticed when I was in Singapore last week was how there is commonality in the world because of American music. I was having breakfast in a room where I was the only American, and the food was from all over the world. There were Chinese, Malay, Indian, Japanese, and British people, but it was Roy Orbison singing "Crying" that I had to listen to. My Indian friend says that American music serves the rest of the world as background music. It is light, cheerful, insipid, and no one is really listening to it.
>
> 2) American music prevents conflict.
>
> This is a very positive way of looking at an issue that has become one of my pet peeves. Through our music, we are healing the world. This may be the only good thing America is doing right now. We are quietly infiltrating the world with sounds that make people feel that they are safe, that life is not a serious enterprise, that everything we do is a little like being at Disneyland®. This afternoon my Indian friend was happily humming along to "White Christmas." America causes trouble and strife, but it also pacifies the world in another way.
>
> 3) America homogenizes the world.
>
> America has done more to make the world the same than any other country I can think of. No one realizes what they are losing when they lose their local identity. I feel this very strongly, that diversity is good for us, that it makes us develop, that everyone in the world eating hamburgers from McDonald's® and drinking Starbuck's® coffee is not a good thing. Everyone speaking English instead of other languages is not a good thing either. Parts of our brains will atrophy. Soon, new ideas for food, beverages, and entertainment will be harder and harder to come by. Let's have a few healthy conflicts and keep the world vibrant.

C Preview Unit 3

After the students have read through the headings and titles for this unit (the easy way: go to the table of contents on page v), they are supposed to choose the title of one of the readings and predict how it will relate to "A Changing World." For example, they may predict that "Lectures vs. Laptops" will be about computers replacing professors.

Health

Kids and Chemicals (pages 154–157)
Elizabeth Guillette

This reading about the dramatic effects of pesticides on five, six, and seven year-olds should scare readers into taking action against environmental dangers.

BEFORE READING (page 154)

A Gather ideas about the topic

Most students have a good sense of the dangers of chemicals in our lives now, particularly for children. They usually know the dangers of chemicals that kill insects and plants, although they may need help with the vocabulary in number 3.

B Ask questions

Possible questions: What effect do toxins have on children? What can we do to protect children from toxins? Why would an anthropologist do this kind of research?

AFTER READING (page 156)

A Find answers to your questions

Suppose one of your questions wasn't answered; you might want to research it. Asking questions before reading focuses our reading on the questions. We may overlook other important information, however, while searching for the answers to our questions.

B Respond to the reading

Annotation has become familiar, we hope. A surprise is the extreme differences between the two groups of children and the number of effects.

C Understand the reading

Note that the drawings are not above the reading; they are in the middle. The drawings reveal the extreme differences. The lists could be put on the board.

HOW IT'S WRITTEN (page 156)

Appreciate the structure

The two paragraphs say what happened in each location and make a contrast between the two. The question at the end of the second paragraph is what the author plans to tell us and works as a "hook" to get us involved in the article. The ending tells us that this is not a story about two unique places, but about the whole world. We hope that students will find the ending effective.

TOPICS FOR WRITING (pages 156–157)

Choose one topic to write about

Topic 1 is similar to some we have suggested previously, but topics 2 and 3 are more in line with community-based research that will involve students in interactions with other community members.

AFTER WRITING (page 157)

Share your writing

We get ideas for how to write from what other people do, how they approach a topic, and what they think of.

. . . .

War on Disease (pages 157–160)
Rick Weiss

Common, age-old diseases, not exotic, unknown ones, cause much death worldwide.

BEFORE READING (page 157)

Think about the topic

Two diseases, SARS and West Nile Virus, have become prevalent since this article was written. Check the CDC or the WHO Web sites for the latest findings on each: <http://www.cdc.gov/>; and <http://www.who.int/en/>.

AFTER READING (page 159)

A Make a personal connection

Depending on where the students are from, one of these diseases will be more meaningful, another more surprising.

B Understand the reading

Possible answers (page 159)

1 The balance between medicine and disease is changing, with disease gaining ground, bringing new dangers.

2 Six diseases, spread in different ways, account for 90 percent of deaths from infectious disease and strike hardest in large, densely populated cities in developing countries.

C Acquire new vocabulary

Here it would be possible to give each group one section of the chart and have them explain the words to the class. Certain scientific words, such as the names of diseases, don't have synonyms, only definitions.

HOW IT'S WRITTEN (page 159)

Notice words of attitude

Words that express a sense of extreme importance or urgency include *lethal, virulent, defenseless, full-blown, four billion,* and *highest risk.*

TOPICS FOR WRITING (page 160)

Choose one topic to write about

Again, the CDC or WHO Web sites and their related links are helpful for the research required to write about these topics.

AFTER WRITING (page 160)

A Add to your essay

This activity refers students back to the new revision technique presented at the end of Unit 2 in the *Adding Information to Essays* toolbox on page 149.

B Share your writing

Take a look at the *Peer Feedback Form* on page 217, and adapt it, if warranted, for this activity or for the future.

No Laughing Matter (pages 161–164)

Sophie Petit-Zerman

This interview offers lots of information on the benefits of laughter. Its format offers a model of one way an interview may be written.

BEFORE READING (page 161)

Preview the reading

Some students may have heard about the connection between laughter and health. Many of our students hadn't. Skimming is introduced in this section. It is an important skill, to be distinguished from reading. Give your students a time limit for skimming this piece (2–3 minutes) and ask what they predict.

AFTER READING (page 163)

A Respond to the reading

The sentences from the text that come up most often in our students' double entry responses are as follows: "Even rats laugh," "Socially dominant individuals . . . use laughter to control their subordinates," "It's undoubtedly the best medicine," and "Staring at computer screens rather than laughing with each other is at odds with what's natural for children."

B Answer questions

The answers to the questions are not hard to find. The purpose is to have students restate material they've read for an audience.

C Connect with another reading

Students will see, we hope, that there is value in the expression of emotions.

HOW IT'S WRITTEN (page 164)

Notice form

"The Model Medic" (pages 124–125) is a profile, with answers to questions worked into the text in the form of direct quotes and paraphrases. "No Laughing Matter" has a Q&A format. In the latter, we never forget that what is written is an interview. In the former, there are moments when we are reliving the interviewee's experiences with her.

TOPICS FOR WRITING (page 164)

Choose one topic to write about

The issue raised in topic 2 will be raised again in "Lectures vs. Laptops" (page 202). Alternative medicine in topic 3 gives students a chance to discuss home remedies as well as cultural differences. An interesting example is on the poison ivy Web site: <http://poisonivy.aesir.com/view/kitchen.html>.

AFTER WRITING (page 164)

Share your writing

This way of responding works well with all writers. An alternative: put the writing on a large piece of posterboard; let readers write anywhere on the posterboard with colored pens.

HEALTH: REVISION (pages 165–166)

This revision section focuses on endings. The exercise after the *Types of Endings* toolbox is a bit difficult to do without the whole text of the essay to guide the students. There may be alternative explanations of what each ending listed does. We suggest you look back at some whole essays with good endings, for example, "Five New Words at a Time" (pages 40–41), "Becoming a Writer" (pages 59–60), "The Search for Identity" (pages 65–66), and "On Turning Fifty" (pages 87–89).

A Choose one essay

Students can do this in class or at home.

B Learn more about endings

Lots of students with limited writing experience, who've probably done only "school writing," have limited knowledge of how to end an essay. They call all endings conclusions but, in fact, usually summarize what they've just said. It is useful to widen their view. Encourage students to practice these different types of endings, not just identify them.

C Revise your essay

As with beginnings, it's good to ask students to experiment with different types of endings. Don't forget the Writers' Tips.

D Share your writing

Depending on the size of the class or other factors, you can break the class into groups.

Environment

The Mercury's Rising (pages 167–171)
Sharon Begley

Warming Seas Prompt Tuvalu Evacuation

The effects of global warming are familiar. But the story of the island country of Tuvalu is probably not, thus, providing a new and specific example. The words the writer chose to describe the Tuvalu situation contribute to making the situation sound dire.

BEFORE READING (page 167)

Gather ideas about the topic

A quick search on the Web produces the following informational sites: Global warming: <http://www.epa.gov/globalwarming>; and Penguins: <http://www.seaworld.org/animal-info/info-books/index.htm>.

AFTER READING (page 169)

A Understand the readings

Although there is some language that students are troubled by in this reading – particularly the word *chow* – they have no trouble coming up with two sentences that indicate the penguins are like the canaries in the coal mines. That is, penguins indicate that something has gone seriously wrong with the temperature of the earth with potentially catastrophic consequences.

Possible answers (page 169)

Consequences of climate change on Tuvalu: evacuation, lowland flooding, salt-water intrusion adversely affecting drinking water and food production, coastal erosion, and more and more destructive hurricanes

B Acquire new vocabulary

Almost every sentence has a useful word.

C Read a map

This activity calls for graphic literacy, considered an important skill today and one on which students may be tested.

HOW IT'S WRITTEN (pages 169–170)

Notice negative connotation

Here we are attempting to give the students a short course in critical linguistics, that is, noticing how the language used to present the topic influences the readers' interpretation of the importance or urgency of the topic.

TOPICS FOR WRITING (pages 170–171)

Choose one topic to write about

Cubing is presented as a way to get started here. It's best to practice this before asking students to try it on their own. Start with something concrete. A penny works well. Then move to a more abstract topic, such as intelligence. Cubing is a great heuristic to take with you to other assignments, other writing, to have the rest of your life.

All three topics require research. When we wrote number 2, we said, "Do some research if necessary." Looking at it again, research seems inevitable.

AFTER WRITING (page 171)

A Check citations

If your school or program requires a format other than APA, please refer your students to a place where they can find out how to use that format correctly.

B Share your writing

Encourage students to be specific about changes they could make to their writing.

· ·

Buzzard (pages 172–174)
Bailey White

This story was one of our favorites in the previous versions of this textbook, *Changes*. It has us looking at nature and nature looking back at us. White reads other stories of hers on National Public Radio, and you can access some of them from the archives on <http://www.npr.org>.

BEFORE READING (page 172)

Pool your knowledge

Understanding what these animals were seemed crucial to the significance of White's piece, hence the matching quiz.

AFTER READING (page 173)

A Respond to the reading

Those yellow eyes come up a lot in the freewriting.

B Understand the main idea

Most students choose the last sentence and say something along the lines of: *We need to remember that the earth belongs to all of its creatures, not just to us.*

HOW IT'S WRITTEN (page 173)

A Notice sentence length

For us, the short sentences at the beginning of the piece give it its dramatic effect, slowing the reader down to appreciate the car coming to a stop.

B Appreciate the structure

Descriptive outlining always needs to be reviewed.

For us, the answer to number 3 is that first White makes us live the story with her. Then she tells us its significance for her and suggests it should be significant to us, too.

TOPICS FOR WRITING (pages 173–174)

Choose one topic to write about

For topic 1, you need to decide if you will accept essays written about pets. A list of endangered species can be found at <http://endangered.fws.gov/>. Topic 3 is rather open-ended.

AFTER WRITING (page 174)

Share your writing

Proofreading at this point helps to prepare the piece for a reader. Of course, they should proofread again after they revise.

....

The Brave Little Parrot (pages 174–179)
Rafe Martin

This retold ancient Buddhist tale is still timely in an environmental context, as well as in other contexts. A fable, it leads directly to writing fables, which we think is useful for writers to master. Martin's Web site is <http://www.rafemartin.com>.

BEFORE READING (pages 174–175)

A Gather ideas about the topic

Students have made the following suggestions about what they could do: stop using tobacco, drinking coffee, or wearing cotton that wasn't grown organically; stop eating hamburgers; use as little water at home as possible; recycle; have your name taken off mailing lists; and plant a tree.

B Prepare for the reading

Many students understood that Martin meant "burning" metaphorically, as in, "being destroyed," and that there might be small acts they could do to save the earth.

AFTER READING (page 177)

A Respond to the reading

If your students don't have the three response questions in their repertoire yet, please refer them to the *Response Questions* toolbox on page 9. We don't go anywhere without them.

B Understand the vocabulary

If done as instructed, this activity can be time consuming. For example, in the fourth paragraph of the text (see below), some of the context clues are in other parts of the text and synonyms are not easy to come up with:

> Darting to the river, she dipped herself in the water. Then she flew back over the now-raging fire. Thick smoke coiled up, filling the sky. Walls of flame shot up, now on one side, now on the other. Pillars of fire leapt before her. Twisting and turning through a mad maze of flame, the little parrot flew bravely on.

Possible answers (page 177)

> **Restatement:** Hurrying to the river, she submerged herself in the water. Then she dashed back over the furious fire. Smoke rose in heavy swirls, covering the sky. Blockades of flames surged, first on one side and then on the other. Towers of fire jumped up in front of her. Swirling through the labyrinth of fire, the parrot flew courageously forward.

C Find the main idea

The main idea: *If we have principles and fight against impossible odds, we just might win.* (If students complain that this only happens in fables, remind them of the story of Erin Brockovich). For information about the trial, not the movie, check the Web site: <http://www.lawbuzz.com/famous_trials/erin_brockovich/erin_brockovich_ch1.htm>.

HOW IT'S WRITTEN (page 178)

Learn about fables

Every culture has its fables, and many of them are about trying to change nature. Most of them include animals that talk and behave like humans. Students usually enjoy sharing these. (Other books on teaching writing offer instructions on how to write fables. One such book is *The Common Sense: What to Write, How to Write It, and Why* by Rosemary Deen.)

TOPICS FOR WRITING (page 178)

Choose one topic to write about

Remind students that fables end with lessons. That's one reason why fables are thought to be helpful to teaching writing: They help the writer make a point, and "good writing" makes a point (according to Donald M. Murray, among others).

AFTER WRITING (page 179)

Share your writing

You might also ask students to reflect on how they wrote their essays. What was easy about the process, what was hard, and so on?

ENVIRONMENT: REVISION (pages 180–181)

In this revision section we introduce Alan Ziegler's concept of the "word boss." Any word that isn't doing its job gets fired and replaced. This is a humorous and helpful way of looking at the work words do.

A Choose one piece of writing

By now students are accustomed to making choices from among their writing pieces.

B Revise your writing

Remind students of the *ARMS* toolbox on page 72 if they seem to need a push to revise.

C Get the words right

Students could work with a partner on this activity. Don't miss the *Writers' Tips*.

D Get feedback

Feel free to adapt the *Peer Feedback Form* (page 217) to suit the class.

E Share your writing

We once posted essays in the hallway at our school. We know students read them because some of the most interesting disappeared. Now we publish a booklet every year and give it away.

Gender Roles

Taming Macho Ways (pages 182–187)

Elvia Alvarado

This excerpt is another favorite of ours. Written in the first person, Alvarado tells it like it is. Her strong, candid voice has authority, and we vicariously experience the conditions and injustices she describes.

BEFORE READING (pages 182–183)

A Gather ideas about the topic

The men in the class may argue that equality depends on exactly what the man is doing in the field. All students may claim there is gender equity in their culture, that this example being agrarian is not representative.

Note on the text: *Macho* is short for *machismo*, a Spanish word defined in *The American Heritage Dictionary* as "an exaggerated sense of masculinity stressing such attributes as physical courage, virility, domination of women, and aggressiveness or violence." It is probably known to most who live in the United States. If your students don't know the term, you may want to explain and supply a synonym, such as "male aggressiveness" or "male dominance."

B Write as you read

There are four breaks, hence, four short writing episodes.

AFTER READING (page 186)

A Share your responses

Women students who have experienced some of what is described in the reading may not be eager to share their logs. Remember their right to pass.

B Make connections

Possible answers (page 186)

Four problems: Women work harder than men; they are usually pregnant or nursing; babies keep them up at night; their husbands beat them

HOW IT'S WRITTEN (page 186)

Think about examples

There is a balanced mix of Alvarado's own observations and the point of view of others that students will notice.

Possible answers (page 186)

Personal examples:

I used to gossip and criticize other women. I used to fight over men . . . I stopped doing these things.

Whenever I'd see the slightest thing I'd go running to my friends . . . Now . . . I wouldn't say anything.

I heard a rumor . . . I made sure to warn the campesinos.

I used to flirt with married men . . . Now I'm more responsible . . .

Observation of others:

I've seen what happens when campesinos organize . . .

So I've noticed that once campesinos have a purpose . . . they drink less. And they stop beating their wives . . .

Students may say that the personal examples help them connect more directly with what Alvarado is saying, that the personal examples are effective.

TOPICS FOR WRITING (page 187)

Choose one topic to write about

Topics 1 and 2 are expository, while topic 3 can be personal. In all three, students should use specific examples and facts to support their claims.

AFTER WRITING (page 187)

Share your writing

This feedback exchange takes time. If partners write on a separate piece of paper, the writer will have something to take home.

. . . .

Women and Work: Around the World, Women Earn Less (pages 187–190)

Newsweek Education Program

You read the title and, if you're a woman, you probably nod yes in agreement. Check out the Web site mentioned in the text, <http://www.aflcio.org/women>, and see if the situation has changed. These days, bulleted texts are common features in various types of writing.

BEFORE READING (page 187)

A Think about the topic

The two previous readings will undoubtedly influence the students' answers to these questions, although some are matters of opinion and will provoke a lively debate.

B Write as you read

Many people read using only yellow markers. Enlarge their palettes. Using two different colors shows the distribution of facts in the article very clearly.

AFTER READING (pages 189–190)

A Respond to the reading

It might be interesting to have partners share some of the similarities and differences in their responses with the class.

B Understand the reading

Paraphrasing should be familiar to your students now.

C Make a graph from the reading

Making a graph has become much easier with online tools. Here are some instructions: <http://apsd.k12.ar.us/goza/ExcelGraphs.html>.

HOW IT'S WRITTEN (page 190)

Appreciate the format

This activity allows students to appreciate the format of this piece and all pieces of writing by identifying the different options available. The bolded headings hold the piece together. "One key result?" could possibly be seen as an opinion. The material under the headings is supporting detail. The last statement under each heading is usually a conclusion. The two shortest sections contain generalizations.

TOPICS FOR WRITING (page 190)

Choose one topic to write about

Topic 1 requires some research in the library or on the Internet, topic 2 might require some interviewing, and topic 3 invites an opinion essay.

AFTER WRITING (page 190)

Ask a partner for feedback

We think it's always important to start with what you like in a person's writing.

Battling Chauvinism to Do a Man's Job (pages 191–193)
InfoChange

Check out the InfoChange Web site, <http://www.infochangeindia.org>. The issues of India are the issues of many places. The Web site has headlines running along the top – a reading exercise in itself.

BEFORE READING (page 191)
Gather ideas about the topic

Depending on the diversity of your students, the differences between what is considered men's work and women's work will surprise your students. They may argue over what changes have taken place in the last ten or twenty years, with mostly women saying not enough changes have happened. The word *chauvinism* is defined in <http://www.m-w.com> as: "excessive or blind patriotism; undue partiality or attachment to a group or place to which one belongs or has belonged; an attitude of superiority toward members of the opposite sex, also: behavior expressive of such an attitude."

AFTER READING (page 192)
A Annotate and summarize the reading

The point of this exercise is to first separate out student's opinions and reactions through annotation, then have them simply state the facts of the piece through their summaries.

B Understand the reading

Some students may point out that it is not only chauvinism but also hierarchical thinking that women had to fight.

HOW IT'S WRITTEN (page 192)
Examine the use of stories

Chamela's specific story is found in the first and fourth paragraphs.

TOPICS FOR WRITING (page 193)
Choose one topic to write about

All of the topics invite students to tell stories from their experiences or reading. You might want to have them look ahead to the end of this unit at the *Choosing Examples* toolbox on page 196 before choosing personal examples to include in their writing.

AFTER WRITING (page 193)

Share your writing

This time the writers choose what they want feedback on: writer's choice.

. . . .

First Lullabye (pages 193–195)

Patricia Kirkpatrick

While this poem was written to celebrate the birth of a daughter, it's about the desire to not know the sex of the child before it's born, to live with the mystery and innocence of the unborn.

BEFORE READING (page 193)

Think about the topic

A surprising number of students agreed with the author and said that they wanted to have the opportunity to imagine having both a son and a daughter and that knowing in advance would deprive them of this chance.

AFTER READING (page 194)

A Understand the reading

The students understand that the writer does not want to know the sex of the baby and uses the pronouns to tell us so.

B Respond to the reading

Double and triple entry responses are easy and relaxed at this point in the course.

HOW IT'S WRITTEN (page 195)

Appreciate the images

The poem has many images for students to respond to. One favorite was "the trembling waterdrop beating inside her."

TOPICS FOR WRITING (page 195)

Choose one topic to write about

The variety in these topics is to invite an opinion in the first topic, a description of tradition and possible change in the second, and an emotional response in the third.

AFTER WRITING (page 195)

Share your writing

This has worked well with instructors or teachers-to-be in faculty development workshops.

GENDER ROLES: REVISION (pages 196–197)

The focus of the revision exercise in this section is on examples. The readings in the section are filled with examples that are sufficient, typical, authentic, and relevant. The description of how to choose examples gives students a chance to see if the examples they chose were appropriate to the topic they were writing about.

A Choose one essay

Again, talking over the two choices with a partner can help a writer make his final decision.

B Think about examples

STAR may help you when responding to students' writing, especially when you realize a student hasn't quite made the point because of insufficient or skewed supporting examples.

C Revise your essay

When trying out titles, refer students to the *Titles* toolbox on page 38.

D Share your writing

Ask the writer to come to the front of the room and sit in the chair of honor.

Into the Future

Kill Your Television (pages 198–201)
Bill Duesing

The author argues convincingly against television.

BEFORE READING (page 198)

Gather ideas about the topic

Students in one class wrote that this was their favorite activity of all! They said they really bonded with their classmates over discussing how much and what

kind of television they watched, especially the group that averaged over 20 hours a week. Needless to say, they could not imagine "killing" their televisions.

AFTER READING (pages 199–200)

A Understand the reading

Again, the combination of annotation and summary helps students separate their own reactions and opinions from those of the author.

Possible answers (page 199)

> **Reasons Duesing uses to convince readers not to watch TV:** we don't use most of our senses; TV could teach us all to think the same way; we may be being damaged physically as well as psychologically; the information we are getting is not objective; and the primary purpose of television is to make us want things.

B Acquire new vocabulary

This activity might be a homework assignment.

HOW IT'S WRITTEN (page 200)

A Notice words that show order

In paragraph three, Duesing begins by telling us that he is going to discuss a book he read called *Four Arguments for the Elimination of Television*, and then he numbers the arguments *one, two, three,* and *four*.

B Observe references to other writers

One of our students had a fairly easy time distinguishing quotes from paraphrases and noticing the punctuation.

C Paraphrase a paragraph

Our students also resisted paraphrasing the eight paragraphs in C, particularly since they had already summarized the article.

D Examine the title

Some didn't think much of the title, its inspiration from a bumper sticker, and its violence. But it did get our attention.

TOPICS FOR WRITING (page 201)

Choose one topic to write about

Given the enthusiasm for the *Before Reading* activity, a number of students may want to write about topic 3 and survey other students about their television watching habits. If this is the case, you might want to help them develop questionnaires.

AFTER WRITING (page 201)

Share your writing

To get students started, it's probably useful to model the *Descriptive Outlining* toolbox on pages 35–36. You might do it for the first paragraph of "Kill Your Television" on the board.

> **Main idea:** Turn off the television set because it's turning us off to the richness of life.

> **Paragraph 1 says:** The writer has been thinking about writing this essay against television for years and has finally decided to do it.

> **Paragraph 1 does:** It introduces the topic with a homely, personal anecdote about the title.

....

Lectures vs. Laptops (pages 201–205)
Ian Ayres

In an Op-Ed piece in *The New York Times*, the author questions the place of laptop computers in the classroom. The letters to the editor that follow are simulated but resemble real letters from the newspaper's readers.

BEFORE READING (page 201)

Preview the reading

Not all students are familiar with *vs.* or *versus*, so you may need to explain that they mean *against*. After skimming, students will write about the conflict between a professor and his students. If they are good skimmers, they will know that the professor is opposed to laptops in the classroom.

AFTER READING (page 204)

A Find pros and cons

Possible answers (page 204)

> **Pros:** multitasking, staying productive, reduces sleepiness, allows research
> **Cons:** video games being played during class, Web surfing, e-mail, stock trading, demoralizing classmates, students not being fully present, engaging in addictive activities

B Understand the reading

The summarizing and discussion of letters can take more than an hour, but it does leave the students with a thorough understanding of the issues involved.

C Acquire new vocabulary

Possible answers (page 204)

> **Some computer-related words:** wired, surf, Internet, Web, e-mail, wireless, laptops, toggle, windows, video game, cybersitter filtering software, virtual chat room, post, surfing, and technological

You could add Solitaire, Minesweeper, and multitasking.

HOW IT'S WRITTEN (pages 204–205)

A Notice words of attitude

Again, we are doing a little critical discourse analysis here. If all of the attitude words were removed, we would have a very different text.

Possible answers (page 204)

> **Some words that indicate the author's attitude:** abusive, increasingly prevalent, deem to be boring, demoralizing, not fully present, addictive, cybersitter filtering software, brazenly resisted, and perversely

B Outline the text

Descriptive outlining reveals how the author develops his argument. The author gives the students' reasons for using laptops in his class in the second to last paragraph so that he can use them to extend his argument in the last paragraph.

TOPICS FOR WRITING (page 205)

Choose one topic to write about

All three of these topics were equally popular among students. For topic 2, we had students arguing in favor of e-mail over the telephone and against automobiles, dishwashers, weed whackers, leaf blowers, and many other features of modern life.

AFTER WRITING (page 205)

Ask for feedback

It's helpful to remind the students of ARMS and of the possibility of asking for feedback since they may feel that they have already used up all of the revising techniques and need to remember that they can be used again and again.

The 20th Century: What's Worth Saving?

(pages 206–210)

Jay Walljasper & Jon Spayde

The editors of *Utne Reader* ask us to reflect on what's worth saving from the twentieth century in a powerful list that includes ideas and social trends as well as inventions.

BEFORE READING (page 206)

Gather ideas about the topic

Many of the items on students' lists are influenced by what they have read in this textbook, not surprisingly. Most of them have at least some of the items in the headings in their lists.

AFTER READING (pages 208–209)

Create a time line

It helps students get a better historical perspective to divide the paragraphs among the groups and make one long time line that includes everything mentioned. Otherwise, some paragraphs are skipped.

HOW IT'S WRITTEN (page 209)

Notice the details

This exercise demonstrates that academic writing uses support from sources.

TOPICS FOR WRITING (page 209)

Choose one topic for writing

If students choose topic 1, direct them to the Web site of the magazine so that they can familiarize themselves with it: <http://www.utne.com/>. At this point, students have a good idea of how to do research and are ready to tackle topic 2. Those with a more philosophical frame of mind can take on topic 3.

AFTER WRITING (page 210)

Share your writing

Here we ask the students to mark each other's writing in the same way they did the reading passage, encouraging them to support their ideas with sources.

Entering the Twenty-First Century (pages 210–213)
Thich Nhat Hanh

The author, a Zen Buddhist monk, writes about entering the twenty-first century. Here is one Web site about him, including how to pronounce his name: <http://www.seaox.com/thich.html>.

BEFORE READING (page 210)

A Gather ideas about the topic

Once students have made two clusters around the words *twenty-first century* and *a changing world*, it is a relatively simple matter to transform the information into a Venn diagram.

B Write as you read

This time the places to pause are not indicated. Ask students to share with one another or the class images that came to mind after each paragraph.

AFTER READING (pages 211–212)

A Respond to the reading

Both this activity and the following one help students examine what they did and did not understand about what they read and how they feel about it.

B Understand the reading

Possible answers (page 212)

> **A sample summary sentence:** We need a way to make good use of all the suffering of the twentieth century so that we can live the next century better.

C Acquire new vocabulary

Students might enjoy making vocabulary quizzes for each other.

HOW IT'S WRITTEN (page 212)

Appreciate the language

Some words associated with a garden include *compost, flowers, fertilize, ground, flower, path,* and *grass.* In order to understand the metaphor, students need to understand the concept of composting, or using old, decaying organic matter to create new enriched soil.

TOPICS FOR WRITING (pages 212–213)

Choose one topic to write about

These topics appear somewhat daunting, but you and students might get some ideas from Web sites on "peace education," which is becoming a field of its own. Here's a United Nations Web site with curriculum, links, quizzes, and more: <http://www.un.org/cyberschoolbus/peace/index.asp>. Go to your favorite search engine, like <http://www.google.com>, and type in "peace education" for other Web sites.

AFTER WRITING (page 213)

A Share your writing

Reading the *Writer's Tip* before starting may motivate students to follow the procedures described here.

B Reflect on writing techniques

This is a chance for students to do some long-range reflecting on their writing processes, that is, to look at what has changed over time in the way they approach writing. In a sense, they are taking stock of what they have learned in your course about how to write. You may want them to share these reflections with the class.

INTO THE FUTURE: REVISION (pages 214–215)

A Choose one piece to revise

Remind students to read the *Writer's Tip*.

B Revise your writing

In this final revision section, students look back at all of the revision pages in the book and remember the importance of revision. If you have time, please let them do this. Revision is difficult for beginning writers, and looking back at these pages may help them remember some of their successes. The final revision suggestions involve logical development and are an important part of making an essay coherent.

C Share your writing

In the final sharing, ask the students to discuss what they have learned about writing. Suggest that they take notes in their journals about what they and others have learned and that they refer to them in their next writing course.